Rob Roy Volume 3

/

ROB ROY.

JTHOR OF "WAVERLEY," "GUY MANNERING," AND

"THE ANTIQUARY."

———

For why ? Because the good old rule
Sufficeth them ; the simple plan,
That they should take, who have the power,
And they should keep who can.
   Rob Roy's Grave.—WORDSWORTH.

———

IN THREE VOLUMES.

VOL. III.

THIRD EDITION.

EDINBURGH:

Printed by James Ballantyne and Co.

R ARCHIBALD CONSTABLE AND CO. EDINBURGH ; AND

LONGMAN, HURST, REES, ORME, AND BROWN,

LONDON.

———

1818.

ROB ROY.

ROB ROY.

CHAPTER I.

Baron of Bucklivie,
May the foul fiend drive ye,
And a' to pieces rive ye,
For building sic a town,
Where there's neither horse meat, nor man's meat, nor a chair
to sit down.

Scottish Popular Rhymes on a bad Inn.

THE night was pleasant, and the moon afforded us good light for our journey. Under her rays, the ground over which we passed assumed a more interesting appearance than during the broad day-light, which discovered the extent of its wasteness. The mingled light and shadows gave it an interest which naturally did not belong to it; and, like the effect of a veil flung over a plain woman, irritated our curiosity on a subject which had in itself nothing gratifying.

The descent, however, still continued, turned, winded, left the more open heaths, and got into steeper ravines, which promised soon to lead us to the banks of some brook or river, and ultimately made good their presage. We found ourselves at length on the bank of a stream, which rather resembled one of my native English rivers than those I had hitherto seen in Scotland. It was narrow, deep, still, and silent; although the imperfect light, as it gleamed on its placid waters, shewed also that we were now among the lofty mountains which formed its cradle. " That's the Forth," said the Baillie, with an air of reverence, which I have observed the Scotch usually pay to their distinguished rivers. The Clyde, the Tweed, the Forth, the Spey, are usually named by those who dwell on their banks with a sort of respect and pride, and I have known duels occasioned by any word of disparagement. I

9

cannot say I have the least quarrel with this sort of harmless enthusiasm. I received my friend's communication with the importance which he seemed to think appertained to it. In fact, I was not a little pleased, after so long and dull a journey, to approach a region which promised to engage the imagination. My faithful squire, Andrew, did not seem to be quite of the same opinion, for he received the solemn information, " That is the Forth," with a " Umph!—an' he had said that's the public-house, it wad hae been mair to the purpose."

The Forth, however, as far as the imperfect light permitted me to judge, seemed to merit the admiration of those who claimed an interest in its stream. A beautiful eminence of the most regular round shape, and clothed with copsewood of hazels, mountain-ash, and dwarf-oak, intermixed with a few magnificent old trees, which, rising above the underwood, exposed their forked and bared branches to the silver-

moonshine, seemed to protect the sources
from which the river sprung. If I could
trust the tale of my companion, which,
while professing to disbelieve every word
of it, he told under his breath, and with an
air of something like intimidation, this hill,
so regularly formed, so beautiful, and gar-
landed with such a beautiful variety of ancient trees and thriving copsewood, was held
by the neighbourhood to contain, within its
unseen caverns, the palaces of the fairies,
a race of airy beings, who formed an inter-
mediate class between men and dæmons,
and who, if not positively malignant to humanity, were yet to be avoided and feared,
on account of their capricious, vindictive,
and irritable disposition.

" They ca' them," said Mr Jarvie, in a
whisper, " *Daoine Schie*, whilk signifies, as
I understand, men of peace ; meaning
thereby to make their gude will. And we
may e'en as weel ca' them that too, Mr Osbaldistone, for there's nae gude in speaking ill o' the laird within his ain bounds."

But he added presently after, on seeing one or two lights which twinkled before us, " It's deceits o' Satan, after a', and I fearna to say it—for we are near the manse now, and yonder are the lights in the Clachan of Aberfoil."

I own I was well pleased at the circumstance to which Mr Jarvie alluded, not so much that it set his tongue at liberty, in his opinion, with all safety to declare his real sentiments with respect to the *Daoine Schie*, or fairies, as that it promised some hours repose to ourselves and our horses, of which, after a ride of fifty miles and upwards, both stood in some need.

We crossed the infant Forth by an old-fashioned stone bridge, very high and very narrow. My conductor, however, informed me, that to get through this deep and important stream, and to clear all its tributary dependencies, the general pass from the Highlands to the southward lay by what was called the Fords of Frew, at all times deep and difficult of passage, and of-

ten altogether unfordable. Beneath these
fords there was no pass of general resort
until so far east as the bridge of Stirling;
so that the river of Forth forms a defensible
line betwixt the Highlands and Lowlands
of Scotland, from its source nearly to the
Frith, or inlet of the ocean, in which it
terminates. The subsequent events which
we have witnessed led me to recal with
attention what the shrewdness of Baillie
Jarvie suggested, in his proverbial expression, that " Forth bridles the wild Highlandman."

About half a mile's riding, after we
crossed the bridge, placed us at the door
of the public-house where we were to pass
the evening. It was a hovel rather worse
as better than that in which we had dined;
but its little windows were lighted up,
voices were heard from within, and all intimated a prospect of food and shelter, to
which we were by no means indifferent.
Andrew was the first to observe that there

was a peeled willow-wand placed across the half-open door of the little inn. He hung back, and advised us not to enter. " For," said Andrew, " some of their chiefs and grit men are birling at the usquebaugh in bye there, and dinna want to be disturbed; and the least we'll get, if we gang ram-stam in on them, will be a broken head, to learn us better havings, if we dinna come by the length of a cauld dirk in our wame, whilk is just as likely."

I looked at the Baillie, who acknowledged, in a whisper, " that the gowk had some reason for singing ance in the year."

Meantime a staring half-clad wench or two came out of the inn and the neighbouring cottages, on hearing the sound of our horses' feet. No one bade us welcome, nor did any one offer to take our horses, from which we had alighted; and to our various enquiries, the hopeless response of " Ha niel Sassenach," was the only answer we could extract. The Baillie, however,.

found (in his experience) a way to make them speak English. "If I gie ye a baw-bee," said he to an urchin of about ten years old, with a fragment of a tattered plaid about him, " will you understand Sassenach ?"

" Ay, ay, that will I," replied the brat, in very decent English.

" Then gang and tell your mammy, my man, there's twa Sassenach gentlemen come to speak wi' her."

The landlady presently appeared, with a lighted piece of split fir blazing in her hand. The turpentine in this species of torch (which is generally dug from out the turf-bogs) makes it blaze and sparkle readily, so that it is often used in the Highlands in lieu of candles. On this occasion such a torch illuminated the wild and anxious features of a female, pale, thin, and rather above the usual size, whose soiled and ragged dress, though aided by a plaid or tartan screen, barely served the purposes of decency, and

certainly not those of comfort. Her black
hair, which escaped in uncombed elf-locks
from under her coif, as well as the strange
and embarrassed look with which she regarded us, gave me the idea of a witch disturbed in the midst of her unlawful rites. She
plainly refused to admit us into the house.
We remonstrated anxiously, and pleaded
the length of our journey, the state of our
horses, and the certainty that there was not
another place where we could be received
nearer than Callander, which the Baillie
stated to be seven Scots miles distant How
many these may exactly amount to in English measurement, I have never been able
to ascertain, but I think the double *ratio*
may be pretty safely taken as a medium
computation. The obdurate hostess treated
our expostulation with contempt.—" Better gang farther than fare waur," she said,
speaking the Scottish Lowland dialect, and
being indeed a native of the Lennox district,—" Her house was taen up wi' them
wadna like to be intruded on wi' strangers,

—She didna ken wha mair might be there— red-coats it might be frae the garrison." (These last words she spoke under her breath, and with very strong emphasis). " The night," she said, " was fair abune head—a night amang the heather wad caller our bloods—we might sleep in our claes as mony a gude blade does in the scabbard —there wasna muckle flow-moss ·in the shaw, if we took up our quarters right, and we might pit up our horses to the hill, naebody wad say naething against it."

" But my good woman," said I, while the Baillie groaned and remained undecided, " it is six hours since we dined, and we have not taken a morsel since. I am positively dying with hunger, and I have no taste for taking up my abode supperless among these mountains of yours. I positively must enter; and make the best apology you can to your guests for adding a stranger or two to their number.—Andrew, you will see the horses put up."

The Hecate looked at me with surprise,

and then ejaculated, " A wilfu' man will
hae his way—them that will to Cupar maun
to Cupar!—To see thae English belly-gods
—he has had ae fu' meal the day already,
and he'll venture life and liberty rather
than he'll want a het supper. Set roast-
beef and pudding on the opposite side o'
the pit o' Tophet, and an Englishman will
mak a spang at it—But I wash my hands
o't.—Follow me, sir," (to Andrew,) " and
I'se shew ye where to pit the beasts."

I own I was somewhat dismayed at my
landlady's expressions, which seemed to be
ominous of some approaching danger. I
did not, however, chuse to shrink back after having declared my resolution, and accordingly I boldly entered the house; and
after narrowly escaping breaking my shins
over a turf back and a salting tub, which
stood on either side of the narrow exterior passage, I opened a crazy half-decay-
ed door, constructed, not of plank, but of
wicker, and, followed by the Baillie, entered into the principal apartment of this
Scottish caravansera.

The interior presented a view which seemed singular enough to southern eyes. The
fire, fed with blazing turf and branches of
dried wood, blazed merrily in the centre;
but the smoke, having no means to escape
but through a hole in the roof, eddied round
the rafters of the cottage, and hung in sable
folds at the height of about five feet from
the floor. The space beneath was kept
pretty clear, by innumerable currents of
air which rushed towards the fire from the
broken pannel of basket-work which served as a door, from two square holes, designed as ostensible windows, through one
of which was thrust a plaid, and through
the other a tattered great-coat; and moreover, through various less distinguishable
apertures in the walls of the tenement,
which, being built of round stones and
turf, cemented by mud, let in the atmosphere at innumerable crevices.

At an old oaken table, adjoining to the
fire, sat three men, guests apparently,
whom it was impossible to regard with
indifference. Two were in the Highland

dress; the one, a little dark-complexion-
ed man, with a lively, quick, and irritable
expression of features, wore the trews, or
close pantaloons, wove out of a sort of
chequered stocking stuff. The Baillie
whispered me, that " he behoved to be a
man of some consequence, for that naebody but their Duinhéwassels wore the
trews ; they were very ill to weave exactly
to their Highland pleasure."

The other mountaineer was a very tall,
strong man, with a quantity of reddish
hair, freckled face, high cheek-bones, and
long chin—a sort of caricature of the national features of Scotland. The tartan
which he wore differed from that of his
companion, as it had much more scarlet in
it, whereas the shades of black and dark-
green predominated in the chequers of the
other. The third, who sate at the same
table, was in the Lowland dress,—a bold,
stout-looking man, with a cast of military
daring in his eye and manner, his riding-
dress showily and profusely laced, and his

cocked hat of formidable dimensions. His
hanger and a pair of pistols lay on the
table before him. Each of the Highlanders had their naked dirks stuck upright in
the board beside him,—an emblem, I was
afterwards informed, but surely a strange
one, that their compotation was not to be
interrupted by any brawl. A mighty pew-
ter measure, containing about an English
quart of usquebaugh, a liquor nearly as
strong as brandy, which the Highlanders
distil from malt, and drink undiluted in
excessive quantities, was placed before these
worthies. A broken glass, with a wooden
foot, served as a drinking cup to the whole
party, and circulated with a rapidity, which,
considering the potency of the liquor, seemed absolutely marvellous. These men spoke
loud and eagerly together, sometimes in
Gaelic, at other times in English. Another Highlander, wrapt in his plaid, reclined on the floor, his head resting on a
stone, from which it was only separated by
a wisp of straw, and slept, or seemed to

sleep, without attending to what was going on around him. He also was probably a stranger, for he lay in full dress, and accoutred with the sword and target, the usual arms of his countrymen when on a journey. Cribs there were of different dimensions beside the walls, formed, some of fractured boards, some of shattered wickerwork or plaited boughs, in which slumbered the family of the house, men, women, and children, their places of repose only concealed by the dusky wreaths of vapour which arose above, below, and around them.

Our entrance was made so quietly, and the carousers I have described were so eagerly engaged in their discussions, that we escaped their notice for a minute or two. But I observed the Highlander who lay beside the fire raise himself on his elbow as we entered, and, drawing his plaid over the lower part of his face, fix his look on us for a few seconds, after which he resumed his recumbent posture, and seemed again to betake himself to the repose which our entrance had interrupted.

We advanced to the fire, which was an agreeable spectacle after our late ride, during the chillness of an Autumn evening among the mountains, and first attracted the attention of the guests who had preceded us, by calling for the landlady. She approached, looking doubtfully and timidly, now at us, now at the other party, and returned a hesitating and doubtful answer to our request to have something to eat.

" She didna ken," she said, " she wasna sure there was ony in the house," and then modified her qualification,—" that is, ony thing fit for the like of us."

I assured her we were indifferent to the quality of our supper; and looking round for means of accommodation, which were not easily to be found, I arranged an old hen-coop as a seat for Mr Jarvie, and turned down a broken tub to serve for my own. Andrew Fairservice entered present-

ly afterwards, and took a place in silence
behind our backs. The natives, as I may
call them, continued staring at us with an
air as if confounded by our assurance, and
we, at least I myself, disguised as well as
we could, under an appearance of indifference, any secret anxiety we might feel concerning the mode in which we were to be
received by our predecessors.

At length, the lesser Highlander, ad-
dressing himself to me, said, in very good
English, and in a tone of great haughtiness,
" Ye make yourself at home, sir, I see."

" I usually do so," I replied, " when I
come into a house of public entertainment."

" And did she na see," said the taller
man, " by the white wand at the door, that
gentlemens had taken up the public-house
on their ain business ?"

" I do not pretend to understand the
customs of this country; but I am yet
to learn," I replied, " how three persons
should be entitled to exclude all other tra-

vellers from the only place of shelter and refreshment for miles round."

"There's nae reason for't, gentlemen," said the Baillie; "we mean nae offence—but there's neither law nor reason for't—but as far as a stoup o' gude brandy wad make up the quarrel, we, being peaceable folk, wad be willing"——

"Damn your brandy, sir!" said the Lowlander, adjusting his cocked-hat fiercely upon his head; "we desire neither your brandy nor your company," and up he rose from his seat. His companions also arose muttering to each other, drawing up their plaids, and snorting and snuffing the air after the manner of their countrymen when working themselves into a passion.

"I tauld ye what wad come, gentlemen," said the landlady, "an' ye wad hae been tauld—get awa wi' ye out o' my house, and make nae disturbance here—there's nae gentleman be disturbed at Jeanie MacAlpine's an' she can hinder. A wheen idle English loons, gaun about the country under cloud o' night, and disturbing honest peaceable gentlemen that are drinking their drap drink at the fire-side."

At another time I should have thought of the old Latin adage,

" Dat veniam corvis, vexat censura columbis"——

But I had not any time for classical quotation, for there was obviously a fray about to ensue, at which, feeling myself indignant at the inhospitable insolence with which I was treated, I was totally indifferent, unless on the Baillie's account, whose person and qualities were ill qualified for such an adventure. I started up, however, on seeing the others rise, and dropped my cloak from my shoulders, that I might be ready to stand on the defensive.

" We are three to three," said the lesser Highlander, glancing his eyes at our party ; " if ye be pretty men, draw ;" and, unsheathing his broadsword, he advanced on me. I put myself in a posture of defence, and, aware of the superiority of my

weapon, a rapier or small-sword, was little
afraid of the issue of the contest. The Baillie behaved with unexpected mettle. As he
saw the gigantic Highlander confront him
with his weapon drawn, he tugged for a second or two at the hilt of his *shabble*, as he
called it; but finding it loth to quit the sheath,
to which it had long been secured by rust
and disuse, he seized, as a substitute, on the
red-hot coulter of a plough which had been
employed in arranging the fire by way of a
poker, and brandished it with such effect,
that at the first pass he set the Highlander's
plaid on fire, and compelled him to keep a
respectful distance till he could get it ex-
tinguished. Andrew, on the contrary, who
ought to have faced the Lowland champion,
had, I grieve to say it, vanished at the very
commencement of the fray. But his antagonist, crying, " Fair play! fair play!"
seemed courteously disposed to take no
share in the scuffle. Thus we commenced
our rencounter on fair terms as to numbers.
My own aim was, to possess myself, if possible, of my antagonist's weapon; but I was

deterred from closing for fear of the dirk
which he held in his left hand, and used in
parrying the thrusts of my rapier. Meantime the Baillie, notwithstanding the success of his first onset, was sorely bested.
The weight of his weapon, the corpulence
of his person, the very effervescence of his
own passions, were rapidly exhausting both
his strength and his breath, and he was almost at the mercy of his antagonist, when
up started the sleeper from the floor on
which he reclined, with his naked sword
and target in his hand, and threw himself
between the discomfited magistrate and
his assailant, exclaiming, " Her nainsell
has eaten the town pread at the Cross o'
Glasgow, and py her troth she'll fight for
Baillie Sharvie at the Clachan of Aberfoil
—tat will she e'en." And, seconding his
words with deeds, this unexpected auxili-
ary made his sword whistle about the ears
of his tall countryman, who, nothing abash-
ed, returned his blows with interest. But
being both accoutred with round targets

made of wood, studded with brass, and covered with leather, with which they readily
parried each other's strokes, their combat
was attended with much more noise and
clatter than serious risk of damage. It
appeared, indeed, that there was more of
bravado than of serious attempt to do us
any injury; for the Lowland gentleman,
who, as I mentioned, had stood aside for
want of an antagonist when the brawl commenced, was now pleased to act the part of
moderator and peace-maker.

"Haud your hands—haud your hands—
aneugh done—aneugh done!—the quarrel's
no mortal. The strange gentlemen have
shewn themselves men of honour, and gi'en
reasonable satisfaction. I'll stand on mine
honour as kittle as ony man, but I hate unnecessary bloodshed."

It was not, of course, my wish to pro-
tract the fray—my adversary seemed equally disposed to sheath his sword—the Baillie, gasping for breath, might be considered as *hors de combat*, and our two sword-

and-buckler men gave up their contest with as much indifference as they had entered into it.

" And now," said the worthy gentleman who acted as umpire, " let us drink and gree like honest fellows—The house will haud us a'. I propose that this good little gentleman that seems sair fourfoughen, as I may say, in this tuilzie, shall send for a tass o' brandy, and I'll pay for another, by way of Archilowe, and then we'll birl our bawbees a' round about, like bre-thren."

" And fa's to pay my new ponny plaid," said the larger Highlander, " wi' a hole burnt in't ane might put a kail-pat through? Saw ever ony body a decent gentleman fight wi' a firebrand before?"

" Let that be nae hinderance," said the Baillie, who had now recovered his breath, and was at once disposed to enjoy the tri-umph of having behaved with spirit, and avoid the necessity of again resorting to such hard and doubtful arbitrement;—" Gin I

hae broken the head," he said, " I sall find
the plaister. A new plaid sall ye hae, and o'
the best—your ain clan-colours, man ; and
ye will tell me where it can be sent t'ye
frae Glasco."

" I needna name my clan—I am of a
king's clan, as is weel kenn'd," said the
Highlander, " but ye may tak a bit o' the
plaid—figh, she smells like a singit sheep's
head !—and that'll learn ye the sett—and
a gentleman, that's a cousin o' my ain, that
carries eggs doun frae Glencroe, will ca'
for't about Martimoes, an' ye will tell her
where ye bide. But, honest gentleman,
neist time ye fight, an' ye hae ony respect
for your athversary, let it be wi' your sword,
man, since ye wear ane, and no wi' thae
het culters and fireprands, like a wild In-
dian."

" Conscience!" replied the Baillie, "every
man maun do as he dow—My sword hasna
seen the light since Bothwell Brigg, when
my father, that's dead and gane, ware it ;
and I kenna weel if it was forthcoming than

5

cither, for the battle was o' the briefest—
At ony rate, it's glewed to the scabbard now
beyond my power to part them; and, finding that, I e'en grippit at the first thing I
could mak a fend wi'. I trow my fighting
days is done, though I like ill to take the
scorn for a' that.—But where's the honest
lad that tuik my quarrel on himsell sae
frankly?—I'se bestow a gill o' aquavitæ on
him, an' I suld never ca' for another."

The champion for whom he looked around
was, however, no longer to be seen. He
had escaped, unobserved by the Baillie, immediately when the brawl was ended, yet
not before I had recognized, in his wild
features and shaggy red-hair, our acquaintance Dougal, the fugitive turnkey of the
Glasgow jail. I communicated this observation in a whisper to the Baillie, who answered, in the same tone, " Weel, weel, I
see that him that ye ken o' said very right.
There *is* some glimmering o' common sense
about that creature Dougal; I maun see
and think o' something will do him some
gude."

Thus saying, he sate down, and fetching one or two deep aspirations, by way of recovering his breath, called to the landlady; " I think, Luckie, now that I find that there's nae hole in my wame, whilk I had muckle reason to doubt frae the doings o' your house, I wad be the better o' something to pit intill't."

The dame, who was all officiousness so soon as the storm had blown over, immediately undertook to broil something comfortable for our supper. Indeed, nothing surprised me more, in the course of the whole matter, than the extreme calmness with which she and her whole household seemed to regard the martial tumult that had taken place. The good woman was only heard to call to some of her assistants, " Steek the door—steek the door!—Kill or be killed, let naebody pass out till they hae paid the lawin." And as for the slumberers in those lairs by the wall, which served the family for beds, they only raised their shirtless bodies to look at the fray, ejaculated, " Oigh! oigh!" in the tone suitable to their respective sex and ages, and were, I believe, fast asleep again ere our swords were well returned to their scabbards.

Our landlady, however, now made a great bustle to get some victuals ready, and, to my surprise, very soon began to prepare for us, in the frying-pan, a savoury mess of venison collops, which she dressed in a manner that might well satisfy hungry men, if not epicures. In the mean time the brandy was placed on the table, to which the Highlanders, however partial to their native strong waters, showed no objection, but much the contrary; and the Lowland gentleman, after the first cup had passed round, became desirous to know our profession, and the object of our journey.

"We are bits o' Glasgow bodies, if it please your honour," said the Baillie, with an affectation of great humility, "travelling to Stirling to get in some siller that is awing us."

I was so silly as to feel a little disconcerted at the unassuming account which
he chose to give of us, but I recollected my
promise to be silent, and allow the Baillie
to manage the matter his own way.   And
really, when I recollected, Will, that I had
not only brought the honest man a long
journey from home, which even in itself
had been some inconvenience, (if I were to
judge from the obvious pain and reluctance
with which he took his seat or arose from
it,) but had also put him within a hair's-
breadth of the loss of his life, I could hardly refuse him such a compliment.   The
spokesman of the other party, snuffing up
his breath through his nose, repeated the
words with a sort of sneer, " Ye Glasgow tradesfolks hae naething to do but to
gang frae the tae end o' the west o' Scotland to the ither, to plague honest folks
that may chance to be awee ahint the hand,
like me."

" If our debtors were a' sic honest gentlemen as I believe you to be, Garschatta-

chin," replied the Baillie, " conscience ! we might save ourselves a labour, for they wad come to seek us."

" Eh ! what ! how !" exclaimed the person whom he had addressed, " as I shall live by bread, (not forgetting beef and brandy,) it's my auld friend Nicol Jarvie, the best man that ever counted doun merks on a band till a distressed gentleman. Were. ye na coming up my way ?—were ye na coming up the Endrick to Garschatta-chin ?"

" Troth no, Maister Galbraith," replied the Baillie, " I had other eggs on the spit —and I thought ye wad be saying I cam to look about the annual rent that's due on the bit heritable band that's between us."

" Damn the annual rent !" said the laird, with an appearance of great heartiness,—, " De'il a word o' business will you or I speak, now that ye're sae near my country. —To see how a trot-cosey and a joseph, can disguise a man—that I suldna ken my auld feal friend the deacon !"

" The baillie, if ye please," resumed my companion ; " but I ken what gars ye mistak—the band was granted to my father that's happy, and he was deacon ; but his name was Nicol as weel as mine.   I dinna mind that there's been a payment of principal sum or annual rent on it in my day, and doubtless that has made the mistake."

" Well, the devil take the mistake and all that occasioned it !" replied Mr Galbraith. " But I am glad ye are a baillie. Gentlemen, fill a brimmer—this is my excellent friend, Baillie Nicol Jarvie's health—I kend him and his father these twenty years. Are ye a' cleared kelty aff?—Fill anither. Here's to his being sune provost—I say provost—. Lord Provost Nicol Jarvie !—and them that affirms there's a man walks the Hie-street o' Glasgow that's fitter for the office, they will do weel not to let me, Duncan Galbraith of Garschattachin, hear them say sae—that's all."   And therewith Duncan Galbraith martially cocked his hat, and placed it on one side of his head with an air of defiance.

The brandy was probably the best recommendation of these complimentary toasts to the two Highlanders, who drunk them without appearing anxious to comprehend their purport. They commenced a conversation with Mr Galbraith in Gaelic, which he talked with perfect fluency, being, as I afterwards learned, a near neighbour to the Highlands.

" I kenn'd that Scant-o'-grace weel aneugh frae the very outset," said the Baillie, in a whisper to me; " but when blude was warm, and swords were out at ony rate, wha kens what way he might hae thought o' paying his debts? it will be lang or he does it in common form. But he's an honest lad, and has a warm heart too; he doesna come aften to the Cross o' Glasgow, but mony a buck and black-cock he sends us doun frae the hills. And I can want my siller weel aneugh. My father the

deacon had a great regard for the family
of Garschattachin."

Supper being now nearly ready, I looked
round for Andrew Fairservice ; but that
trusty follower had not been seen by any
one since the beginning of the rencontre.
The hostess, however, said that she believed our servant had gone into the stable,
and offered to light me to the place, saying
that " no entreaties of the bairns or hers
could make him give any answer ; and that
truly she cared na to gang into the stable
hersell at this hour. She was a lone woman, and it was weel kenn'd how the
Brownie of Ben-ye-gask guided the gudewife of Ardnagowan ; and it was aye judged there was a Brownie in our stable,
which garr'd me gie ower keeping an host-
ler." ·

As, however, she lighted me towards the
miserable hovel into which they had crammed our unlucky steeds, to regale themselves
on hay, every fibre of which was as thick

as an ordinary quill, she plainly shewed me
that she had another reason for drawing
me aside from the company than that which
her words implied. " Read that," she said,
slipping a piece of paper into my hand as
we arrived at the door of the shed; " I
bless God I am rid o't. Between sogers
and Saxons, and katerans and cattle-lifters,
and hership and bluidshed, an honest woman wad live quieter in hell than on the
Highland line."

So saying, she put the pine torch into
my hand, and returned into the house.

CHAPTER II.

Bagpipes, not lyres, the Highland hills adorn,
Maclean's loud hollo, and MacGregor's horn.
John Cooper's Reply to Allan Ramsay.

I STOPPED in the entrance of the stable, if indeed a place be entitled to that name where horses were stowed away along with goats, poultry, pigs, and cows, under the same roof with the mansion-house; although, by a degree of refinement unknown to the rest of the hamlet, and which I afterwards heard was imputed to an overpride on the part of Jeany Mac-Alpine, our landlady, the apartment was accommodated with an entrance different from that used by her biped customers. By the light of my torch, I decyphered the

following billet, written on a wet, crum-
pled, and dirty piece of paper, and addressed, " For the honoured hands of Mr
F. O. a Saxon young gentleman—These."
The contents were as follows :

" Sir,

" There are night-hawks abroad, so that
I cannot give you and my respected kinsman, B. N. J., the meeting at the Clachan
of Aberfoil, whilk was my purpose. I pray
you to avoid unnecessary communication
with those you may find there, as it may
give future trouble. The person who gives
you this is faithful, and may be trusted, and
will guide you to a place where, God willing, I may safely give you the meeting,
when I trust my kinsman and you will visit my poor house, where, in despite of my
enemies, I can still promise sic cheer as ane
Hielandman may gie his friends, and where
we will drink a solemn health to a certain
D. V. and look to certain affairs whilk I

hope to be your aidance in ; and I rest, as is wont among gentlemen, your servant to command,   R. M. C."

I was a good deal mortified at the purport of this letter, which seemed to adjourn to a more distant place and date the service which I had hoped to receive from this man Campbell. Still, however, it was some comfort to know that he continued to be in my interest, since without him I could have no hope of recovering my father's papers. I resolved, therefore, to obey his instructions ; and, observing all caution before the guests, to take the first good opportunity I could find to obtain from the landlady directions how I was to obtain a meeting with this mysterious person.

My next business was to seek out Andrew Fairservice, whom I called several times by name, without receiving any answer, surveying the stable all around, at the same time, not without risk of setting

the premises on fire, had not the quantity
of wet litter and mud so greatly counter-
balanced two or three bunches of straw
and hay. At length my repeated cries of
" Andrew Fairservice—Andrew! Fool—
Ass, where are you ?" produced a doleful
" Here," in a groaning tone, which might
have been that of the Brownie itself. Guided by this sound, I advanced to the corner
of a shed, where, ensconced in the angle of
the wall, behind a barrel full of the feathers
of all the fowls which had died in the cause
of the public for a month past, I found the
manful Andrew ; and, partly by force,
partly by command and exhortation, compelled him forth into the open air. The
first words he spoke were, " I am an honest lad, sir."

" Who the devil questions your honesty ?" said I; " or what have we to do
with it at present ? I desire you to come
and attend us at supper."

" Yes," reiterated Andrew, without apparently understanding what I said to him,

" I am an honest lad, whatever the Baillie may say to the contrary. I grant the warld and the warld's gear sits ower near my heart whiles, as it does to mony a ane —But I am an honest lad; and, though I spak o' leaving ye in the muir, yet God knows it was far frae my purpose, but just like idle things folk says when they're driving a bargain, to get it as far to their ain side as they can—And I like your honour weel for sae young a lad, and I wadna part wi' ye lightly."

" What the deuce are you driving at now?" I replied. " Has not every thing been settled again and again to your satisfaction? And are you to talk of leaving me every hour, without either rhyme or reason?"

" Ay, but I was only making fashion before," replied Andrew; " but it's come on me in sair earnest now—Lose or win, I daur gae nae farther wi' your honour; and, if ye'll take my foolish advice, ye'll bide by a broken tryste, rather than gang for-

ward yoursel—I hae a sincere regard for
ye, and I'm sure ye'll be a credit to your
friends if ye live to saw out your wild aits,
and get some mair sense and steadiness—
But I can follow ye nae farther, even if ye
suld founder and perish from the way for
lack of guidance and counsel—to gang into
Rob Roy's country is a mere tempting o'
Providence."

" Rob Roy ?" said I, in some surprise ;
" I know no such person. What new trick
is this, Andrew ?"

" It's hard," said Andrew—" very hard,
that a man canna be believed when he
speaks Heaven's truth, just because he's
whiles owercome, and lies a little when
there's necessary occasion. Ye needna ask
whae Rob Roy is, the reiving lifter that
he is—God forgie me! I hope naebody
hears us—when ye hae a letter frae him in
your pouch. I heard ane o' his gillies bid
that auld rudas jaud of a gudewife gie ye
that. They thought I didna understand

their gibberish ; but, though I canna speak
it muckle, I can gie a gude guess at what
I hear them say—I never thought to hae
tauld ye that, but in a fright a' things come
out that suld be keepit in. O, Maister
Frank, a' your uncle's follies, and a' your
cousins' pliskies, were naething to this !—
Drink clean cap-out, like Sir Hildebrand ;
begin the blessed morning with brandy
sops, like Squire Percie ; swagger, like
Squire Thorncliffe ; rin wud amang the
lasses, like Squire John ; gamble, like Rich-
ard ; win souls to the pope and the deevil,
like Rashleigh ; rive, rant, break the Sab-
bath, and do the pope's bidding, like them
a' put thegither—But merciful Providence !
take care o' your young bluid, and gang
nae near Rob Roy !"

Andrew's alarm was too sincere to permit me to suppose he counterfeited. I
contented myself, however, with telling
him, that I meant to remain in the ale-
house that night, and desired to have the

horses well-looked after. As to the rest, I charged him to observe the strictest silence upon the subject of his alarm, and he might rely upon it I would not incur any serious danger without due precaution. He followed me with a dejected air into the house, observing between his teeth, " Man suld be served afore beast—I haena had a morsel in my mouth but the rough legs o' that auld moorcock this hale blessed day."

The harmony of the company seemed to have suffered some interruption since my departure, for I found Mr Galbraith and my friend the Baillie high in dispute.

" I'll hear nae sic language," said Mr Jarvie, as I entered, " respecting the Duke o' Argylle and the name o' Campbell. He's a worthy public-spirited nobleman, and a credit to the country, and a friend and benefactor to the trade o' Glasgow."

" I'll say naething against MacCallummore and the Slioch-nan-Diarmid," said the lesser Highlander, laughing. " I live on the wrang side of Glencroe to quarrel with Inverara."

" Our loch ne'er saw the Campbell lymphads," * said the bigger Highlander. " She'll speak her mind and fear naebody —She doesna value a Cawmil mair as a Cowan, and ye may tell MacCallummore that Allan Iverach said sae—It's a far cry to Lochow."†

Mr Galbraith, on whom the repeated pledges which he had quaffed had produced some influence, slapped his hand on the table with great force, and said, in a stern voice, " There's a bloody debt due by that family, and they will pay it one day—The banes of a loyal and a gallant Grahame hae lang rattled in their coffin

---

* *Lymphads.* The galley which the family of Argyle and others of the Clan-Campbell carry in their arms.

† Lochow and the adjacent districts formed the original seat of the Campbells. The expression of a " far cry to Lochow," was proverbial.

for vengeance on thae Dukes of Guile and Lords for Lorn. There ne'er was treason in Scotland but a Cawmil was at the bottom o't; and now that the wrang side's uppermost, wha but the Cawmils for keeping down the right? But this warld winna last lang, and it will be time to sharp the maiden for shearing o' craigs and thrapples. I hope to see the auld rusty lass linking at a bluidy harst again."

" For shame, Garschattachin !" exclaimed the Baillie ; " fye for shame, sir ; wad ye say sic things before a magistrate, and bring yoursell into trouble?—How d'ye think to mainteen your family and satisfy your creditors (mysell and others), if ye gang on in that wild way, which cannot but bring you under the law, to the prejudice of a' connected wi' ye ?"

" Damn my creditors," retorted the gallant Galbraith, " and you, if ye be ane of them. I say there will be a new warld sune—And we shall hae nae Cawmils cocking their bonnet sae hie, and hound-

ing their dogs where they daurna come
themsells, nor protecting thieves, and murderers, and oppressors, to harry and spoil
better men and mair loyal clans than themsells."

The Baillie had a great mind to have
continued the dispute, when the savoury
vapour of the broiled venison, which our
landlady now placed before us, proved so
powerful a mediator, that he betook himself to his trencher with great eagerness,
leaving the strangers to carry on the debate
among themselves.

" And tat's true," said the taller Highlander, whose name I found was Stuart,
" for we suldna be plagued and worried
here wi' meetings to pit down Rob Roy, if
the Cawmils didna gae him refutch. I was
ane o' thirty o' my ain name—part Glenfinlas, and part men that came down frae
Appine. We shased the MacGregors as
ye wad shase rae-deer till we came into
Glenfalloch's country, and the Cawmils
raise and wadna let us pursue nae farder,

and sae we lost our labour; but her wad
gie twa and a plack to be as near Rob as
she was tat day."

It seemed to happen very unfortunately,
that in every topic of discourse which these
gentlemen introduced, my friend the Baillie found some matter of offence. " Ye'll
forgie me speaking my mind, sir; but ye
wad maybe hae gien the best ball in your
bonnet to hae been as far awa frae Rob as
ye are e'en now—Odd, my het pleugh-
culter wad hae been naething to his claymore."

" She had better speak nae mair about
her culter, or, by G—, her will gar her eat
her words, and twa handfulls o' cauld steel
to drive them ower wi'." And, with a most
inauspicious and menacing look, the mountaineer laid his hand on his dagger.

" We'll hae nae quarrelling, Allan," said
his shorter companion; " and if the Glasgow gentleman has ony regard for Rob
Roy, he'll maybe see him in cauld irons
the night, and playing tricks on a tow the

morn; for this country has been ower lang plagued wi' him, and his race is near-hand run—And it's time, Allan, we were ganging to our lads."

" Hout awa, Inverashalloch," said Galbraith. " Mind the auld saw, man— It's a bauld moon, quoth Bennygask. Another pint, quoth Lesly; we'll no start for another chappin."

" I hae had chappins aneugh," said Inverashalloch; " I'll drink my quart of usquebaugh or brandy wi' ony honest fellow, but the de'il a drap mair when I hae wark to do in the morning. And, in my puir thinking, Garschattachin, ye had better be thinking to bring up your horsemen to the Clachan before day, that we may a' start fair."

" What the devil are ye in sic a hurry for?" said Garschattachin; " meat and mess never hindered wark. An it had been my directing, deil a bit o' me wad hae fashed ye to come down the glens to help us. The garrison and our ain horse could hae ta'en Rob Roy easily aneugh. There's the hand," he said, holding up his own, " should lay him on the green, and never ask a Hielandman o' ye a' for his help."

" Ye might hae loot us bide still where we were, then," said Inverashalloch. " I didna come sixty miles without being sent for. But an ye'll hae my opinion, I redd ye keep your mouth better steekit, if ye hope to speed. Shored folk live lang, and sae may him ye ken o'. The way to catch a bird is no to fling your bannet at her. And also thae gentlemen hae heard some things they suldna hae heard, an the brandy had-na been ower bauld for your brain, Major Galbraith. Ye needna cock your hat and bully, man, wi' me, for I will not bear it."

" I hae said it," said Galbraith, with a solemn air of drunken gravity, " that I will quarrel no more this night either with cloth or tartan. When I am off duty, I'll quarrel with you or ony man in the Hielands or

Lowlands, but not on duty—no—no.—
I wish we heard o' these red-coats. If it
had been to do ony thing against King
James, we wad haë seen them lang syne—
but when it's to keep the peace o' the
country, they can lie as lound as their
neighbours."

As he spoke, we heard the measured
footsteps of a body of infantry on the
march ; and an officer, followed by two or
three files of soldiers, entered the apartment. He spoke in an English accent,
which was very pleasant to my ears, now
so long accustomed to the varying brogue
of the Highland and Lowland Scotch.

" You are, I suppose, Major Galbraith,
of the squadron of Lennox Militia, and
these are the two Highland gentlemen
with whom I was appointed to meet in
this place ?"

They assented, and invited the officer
to take some refreshments, which he declined.

" I have been too late, gentlemen, and
am desirous to make up time. I have or-

ders to search for and arrest two persons guilty of treasonable practices."

" We'll wash our hands o' that," said Inverashalloch. " I came here wi' my men to fight against the red MacGregor that killed my cousin, seven times removed, Duncan Maclaren in Invernenty; but I will hae naething to do touching honest gentlemen that may be gaun through tne country on their ain business."

" Nor I neither," said Iverach.

Major Galbraith took up the matter more solemnly, and, premising his oration with a hiccup, spoke to the following purpose :

" I shall say naething against King George, Captain, because, as it happens, my commission may rin in his name—but one commission being good, sir, does not make another bad ; and some think that James may be just as gude a name as George. There's the king that is—and there's the king that should of right be—I say, an honest man may and should be loyal to them both, Captain. But I am of the Lord-Lieutenant's opinion for the time, as it becomes a militia officer and a depute-lieutenant,—and about treason and all that, it's lost time to speak of it—least said is sunest mended."

" I am sorry to see how you have been employing your time, sir," replied the English officer,—as indeed the honest gentleman's reasoning had a strong relish of the liquor he had been drinking,—" and I could wish, sir, it had been otherwise on an occasion of this consequence. I would recommend to you to try to sleep for an hour.—Do these gentlemen belong to your party ?"—looking at the Baillie and me, who, engaged in eating our supper, had paid little attention to the officer on his entrance.

" Travellers, sir," said Galbraith—" lawful travellers by sea and land, as the prayer-book hath it."

" My instructions," said the Captain, taking a light to survey us closer, " are to place under arrest an elderly and a young person, and I think these gentlemen answer nearly the description."

" Take care what you say, sir," said Mr Jarvie ; " it shall not be your red coat, nor your laced hat shall protect you, if you put any affront on me. I'se convene ye baith in an action of scandal and false imprisonment—I am a free burgess and a magistrate o' Glasgow ; Nicol Jarvie is my name, sae was my father's afore me—I am a baillie, be praised for the honour, and my father was a deacon."

" He was a prick-eared cur," said Major Galbraith, " and fought again the King at Bothwell Brigg."

" He paid what he ought and what he bought, Mr Galbraith," said the Baillie, " and was an honester man than ever stude on your shanks."

" I have no time to attend to all this," said the officer ; " I must positively detain you, gentlemen, unless you can produce some respectable security that you are loyal subjects."

" I ᴗdesire to be carried before some civil magistrate," said the Baillie—"the sherra or the judge of the bounds—I am not obliged to answer every red-coat that speers questions at me."

" Well, sir, I shall know how to manage you if you are silent—And you, sir," (to me) " what may your name be?"

" Francis Osbaldistone, sir."

" What! a son of Sir Hildebrand Osbaldistone, of Northumberland?"

" No, sir," interrupted the Baillie; " a son of the great William Osbaldistone, of the house of Osbaldistone and Tresham, Crane-Alley, London."

" I am afraid, sir," said the officer, "your name only increases the suspicions against you, and lays me under the necessity of requesting that you will give up what papers you have in charge."

I observed the Highlanders look anxiously at each other when this proposal was made. " I had none," I replied, " to surrender."

The officer commanded me to be disarmed and searched. To have resisted would have been madness. I accordingly gave up my arms, and submitted to a search, which was conducted as civilly as an operation of the kind well could. They found nothing except the note which I had received that night through the hand of the landlady.

"This is different from what I expected," said the officer; "but it affords us good grounds for detaining you. Here I find you in written communication with the outlawed robber, Robert MacGregor Campbell, who has been so long the plague of this district—How do you account for that?"

"Spies of Rob!" said Inverashalloch—"we wad serve them right to strap them up till the neist tree."

"We are gaun to see after some gear o' our ain, gentlemen," said the Baillie "that's fa'en into his hands by accident—there's nae law again a man looking after his ain, I hope?"

" How did you come by this letter?" said the officer, addressing himself to me.

I could not think of betraying the poor woman who had given it to me, and remained silent.

" Do you know any thing of it, fellow ?" said the officer, looking at Andrew, whose jaws were chattering like a pair of castanets at the threat thrown out by the Highlander.

" O ay, I ken a' about it—It was a Hieland loon gied the letter to that langtongued jaud the gudewife there—I'll be sworn my maister kenn'd naething about it. But he's wilfu' to gang up the hills and speak wi' Rob ; and O, sir, it wad be a charity just to send a wheen o' your redcoats to see him safe back to Glasgow again, whether he will or no—And ye can keep Mr Jarvie as lang as ye like—He's responsible eneugh for ony fine ye may lay on him—and so's my master, for that matter—for me, I'm just a puir gardner lad, and no worth your steering."

" I believe," said the officer, " the best thing I can do is to send these persons to the garrison under an escort. They seem to be in immediate correspondence with the enemy, and I shall be in no respect snswerable for suffering them to be at liberty.— Gentlemen, you will consider yourselves as my prisoners. So soon as dawn approaches I will send you to a place of security. If you be the persons you describe yourselves, it will soon appear, and you will sustain no great inconvenience from being detained a day or two.—I can hear no remonstrances," he continued, turning away from the Baillie, whose mouth was open to address him, " the service I am on gives me no time for idle discussions."

" Aweel—aweel, sir," said the Baillie, " you're welcome to a tune on your ain fiddle, but see if I dinna gar ye dance till't afore a's dune."

An anxious consultation now took place between the officer and the Highlanders,

but carried on in so low a tone, that it was
impossible to catch the sense. So soon as
it was concluded they all left the house.
At their departure, the Baillie thus expressed himself : " Thae Hielandmen are
o' the westland clans, and just as light-
handed as their neighbours, an a' tales be
true, and yet ye see thae hae brought them
frae the head o' Argyleshire to make war
wi' puir Rob for some auld ill-will that they
hae at him and his sirname—And there's
the Grahames, and the Buchanans, and the
Lennox gentry, a' mounted and in order.—
It's weel kenn'd their quarrel—and I dinna
blame them—naebody likes to lose his
kye—and then there's sodgers, puir things,
hoyed out frae the garrison at a' body's
bidding—Puir Rob will hae his hands fu'
by the time the sun comes ower the hill.
Weel—it's wrang, for a magistrate to be
wishing ony thing again the course o' justice, but deil o' me an' I wad break my
heart to hear that Rob had gien them a'
their paiks."

CHAPTER III.

—————— General,
Hear me, and mark me well, and look upon me
Directly in my face—my woman's face—
See if one fear, one shadow of a terror,
One paleness dare appear, but from my anger,
To lay hold on your mercies.

Bonduca.

WE were permitted to slumber out the remainder of the night in the best manner that the miserable accommodations of the ale-house permitted. The Baillie, fatigued with his journey and the subsequent scenes, less interested also in the event of our arrest, which to him could only be a matter of temporary inconvenience, perhaps less nice than habit had rendered me about the cleanliness or decency of his couch, tumbled himself into one of the cribs which I

have already described, and soon was heard
to snore soundly. A broken sleep, snatched by intervals, while I rested my head upon the table, was my only refreshment. In
the course of the night I had occasion to
observe, that there seemed to be some
doubt and hesitation in the motions of the
soldiery. Men were sent out, as if to obtain intelligence, and returned apparently
without bringing any satisfactory information to their commanding officer. He was
obviously eager and anxious, and again
dispatched small parties of two or three
men, some of whom, as I could understand
from what the rest whispered to each other,
did not return again to the Clachan or village.

The morning had broken, when a corporal and two men rushed into the hut,
dragging after them, in a sort of triumph,
a Highlander, whom I immediately recog-
nised as my acquaintance the ex-turnkey.
The Baillie, who started up at the noise
with which they entered, immediately made

the same discovery, and exclaimed, " Mercy on us! they hae grippit the puir creature Dougal—Captain, I will put in bail—sufficient bail for that Dougal creature."

To this offer, dictated, undoubtedly, by a grateful recollection of the late interference of the Highlander in his behalf, the Captain only answered, by requesting Mr Jarvie to " mind his own affairs, and remember that he was himself for the present a prisoner."

" I take you to witness, Mr Osbaldistone," said the Baillie, who was probably better acquainted with the process in civil than in military cases, " that he has refused sufficient bail. It's my opinion that the creature Dougal will have a good action of wrongous imprisonment and damages again him, under the Act seventeen hundred and one, and I'll see the creature righted."

The officer, whose name I understood was Thornton, paying no attention to the Baillie's threats or expostulations, instituted a very close enquiry into Dougal's life and conversation, and compelled him to admit, though with apparent reluctance, the successive facts,—that he knew Rob Roy MacGregor—that he had seen him within these twelve months—within these 'six' months—within this month—within' this week; in fine, that he had parted from him only an hour ago. All this detail came like drops of blood from the prisoner, and was, to all appearance, only extorted by the threat of an halter and the next tree, which Captain Thornton assured him should be his doom, if he did not give direct and special information.

"And now, my friend," said the officer, "you will please inform me how many men your master has with him at present."
Dougal looked in every direction except at the querist, and began to answer, " She canna just be shure about that."

"Look at me, you Highland dog," said the officer, " and remember your life depends on your answer. How many rogues

5

had that outlawed scoundrel with him when
you left him ?"

" Ou, no aboon sax rogues when I was
gane."

" And where are the rest of his ban-
ditti ?"

" Gane wi' the Lieutenant agane ta
westland carles."

" Against the westland clans ?" said the
Captain. " Umph—that is likely enough;
and what rogue's errand were you dispatched upon ?"

" Just to see what your honour and ta
gentlemen red-coats were doing doun here
at ta Clachan."

" The creature will prove fause-hearted
after a'," said the Baillie, who by this time
had planted himself close behind me; " it's
lucky I didna pit mysell to expences anent
him."

" And now, my friend," said the Captain,
" let us understand each other. You have
confessed yourself a spy, and should string
up to the next tree—but come, if you will
do me one good turn, I will do you ano-

ther. You, Donald—you shall just in the
way of kindness carry me and a small party
to the place where you left your master, as
I wish to speak a few words with him on
serious business ; and I'll let you go about
your business, and give you five guineas to
boot."

" Oigh ! oigh !" exclaimed Dougal, in
the extremity of distress and perplexity,
" she canna do tat—she canna do tat—
she'll rather be hanged."

" Hanged, then, you shall be, my
friend," said the officer ; " and your blood
be on your own head.—Corporal Cramp,
do you play Provost-Marshal—away with
him."

The corporal had confronted poor Dougal for some time, ostentatiously twisting
a piece of cord which he had found in the
house into the form of a halter. He now
threw it about the culprit's neck, and, with
the assistance of two soldiers, had dragged
Dougal as far as the door, when, overcome
with the terror of immediate death, he ex-

claimed, " Shentlemans, stops—stops !—
She'll do his honour's bidding—stops !"

" Awa' wi' the creature," said the Baillie,
" he deserves hanging mair now than ever
—awa' wi' him, corporal—why dinna ye
take him awa' ?"

" It's my belief and opinion, honest gentleman," said the corporal, " that if you
were going to be hanged yourself, you
would be in no such d——d hurry."

This bye dialogue prevented my hearing
what passed between the prisoner and Captain Thornton, but I heard the former sni-
vel out, in a very subdued tone, " And
ye'll ask her to gang nae farther than just
to shew ye where the MacGregor is ?—
Ohon ! ohon !"

" Silence your howling, you rascal—
No; I give you my word I will ask you
to go no farther.—Corporal, make the
men fall-in in front of the houses. Get
out these gentlemen's horses ; we must
carry them with us. I cannot spare any
men to guard them here.—Come, my lads,
get under arms."

The soldiers' bustled about, and were ready to move. We were led out, along with Dougal, in the capacity of prisoners. As we left the hut, I heard our companion in captivity remind the Captain of " 'ta foive kuineas."

"Here they are for you," said the officer, putting gold into his hands ; " but observe, that if you attempt to mislead me, I will blow your brains out with my own hand."

" The creature," said the Baillie, " is waur than I judged him—it is a warldly and a perfidious creature—O the filthy lucre of gain that men gi'es themsels up to ! My father the deacon used to say, the penny siller slew mair souls than the naked sword slew bodies."

The landlady now approached, and demanded payment of her reckoning, including all that had been quaffed by Major Galbraith and his Highland friends. The English officer remonstrated, but Mrs MacAlpine declared, if she " hadna trusted to his honour's name being used in their company, she wad never hae drawn them a stoup o' liquor; for Mr Galbraith, she might see him again, or she might no, but weel did she wot she had sma' chance of seeing her siller—and she was a puir widow, had naething but her custom to rely on."

Captain Thornton put a stop to her remonstrances by paying the charge, which was only a few English shillings, though the amount sounded very formidable in Scottish denominations. The generous officer would have included Mr Jarvie and me in this general acquittance; but the Baillie, disregarding an intimation from the landlady, to " make as muckle of the Inglishers as we could, for they were sure to gie us plague eneugh," went into a formal accounting respecting our share of the reckoning, and paid it accordingly. The Captain took the opportunity to make us some slight apology for detaining us. " If we were loyal and peaceable subjects," he said, " we would not regret being stopped for a day, when it was essential to the king's service ; if otherwise, he was acting according to his duty."

We were compelled to accept an apology which it would have served no purpose to refuse, and we sallied out to attend him on his march.

I shall never forget the delightful sensation with which I exchanged the dark, smoky, smothering atmosphere of the Highland hut, in which we had passed the night so uncomfortably, for the refreshing fragrance of the morning air, and the glorious beams of the rising sun, which, from a tabernacle of purple and golden clouds, were darted full on such a scene of natural romance and beauty as had never before greeted my eyes.   To the left lay the valley, down which the Forth wandered on its easterly course, surrounding the beautiful detached hill, with all its garland of woods. On the right, amid a profusion of thickets, knolls, and crags, lay the bed of a broad mountain lake, lightly curled into tiny waves by the breath of the morning breeze, each glittering in its course under the influence of the sun-beams. High hills, rocks, and banks, waving with natural forests of birch and oak, formed the borders of this enchanting sheet of water; and, as their leaves rustled to the wind and twinkled in the sun, gave to the depth of solitude a sort of life and vivacity. Man alone seemed to be placed in a state of inferiority, in a scene where all the ordinary features of nature were raised and exalted. The miserable little *bourocks*, as the Baillie termed them, of which about a dozen formed the village called the Clachan of Aberfoil, were composed of loose stones, cemented by clay instead of mortar, and thatched by turfs, laid rudely upon rafters formed of native and unhewn birches and oaks from the woods around. The roofs approached the ground so nearly, that Andrew Fairservice observed we might have ridden over the village the night before, and never found out we were near it, unless our horses' feet had " gane thro' the riggin."

From all we could see, Mrs MacAlpine's

house, miserable as were the quarters it afforded, was still by far the best in the hamlet; and I dare say (if my description gives
you any curiosity to see it) you will hardly
find it much improved at the present day,
for the Scotch are not a people who speed-
ily admit innovation, even when it comes
in the shape of improvement.*

  The inhabitants of these miserable dwellings were disturbed by the noise of our departure; and as our party of about twenty
soldiers drew up in rank before marching
off, we were reconnoitred by many a bel-

---

* I do not know how this might stand in Mr Osbaldistone's day; but I can assure the reader, whose
curiosity may lead him to visit the scenes of these romantic adventures, that the Clachan of Aberfoil now
affords a very comfortable little inn. If he chances to
be a Scottish antiquary, it will be an additional recommendation to him, that he will find himself in the vicinity, of the Rev. Dr Grahame, minister of the gospel
at Aberfoil, whose urbanity, in communicating information on the subject of national antiquities, is scarce
exceeded even by the stores of legendary lore which
he has accumulated.

dame from the half-opened door of her cottage. As these sybils thrust forth their grey heads, imperfectly covered with close caps of flannel, and showed their shrivelled brows, and long skinny arms, with various gestures, shrugs, and muttered expressions in Gaelic addressed to each other, my imagination recurred to the witches of Macbeth, and I thought I read in the features of these crones the malevolence of the weird sisters. The little children also, who began to crawl forth, some quite naked, and others very imperfectly covered with tatters of tartan stuff, clapped their tiny hands, and grinned at the English soldiers, with an expression of national hate and malignity which seemed beyond their years. I remarked particularly that there were no men, nor so much as a boy of ten or twelve years old, to be seen among the inhabitants of a village which seemed populous in proportion to its extent; and the idea certainly occurred to me, that we were likely to receive from them, in the course of our journey, more effectual tokens of ill-will than those which lowered on the visages and dictated the murmurs of the women and children.

It was not until we commenced our march that the malignity of the elder persons of the community broke forth into expressions. The last file of men had left the village, to pursue a small broken track, formed by the sledges in which the natives transported their peats and turfs, and which led through the woods which fringed the lower end of the lake, when a shrilly sound of female exclamation mixed with the screams of children, the hooping of boys, and the clapping of hands with which the Highland dames enforce their notes, whether of rage or lamentation. I asked Andrew, who looked as pale as death, what all this meant.

" I doubt we'll ken that ower sune," said he. " Means ?—It means that the Highland wives are cursing and banning the red-coats, and wishing ill-luck to them,

and ilka ane that ever spoke the Saxon
tongue. I have heard wives flyte in England and Scotland—it's nae marvel to hear
them flyte ony gate — but sic ill-scrapit
tongues as thae Hieland carlines'—and sic
grewsome wishes, that men should be
slaughtered like sheep — and that they
should lapper their hands to the elbows
in their heart's blude—and that they suld
dee the death of Walter Cuming of Gui-
yock, wha hadna as muckle o' him left thegither as would supper a messan-dog—sic
awsome language as that I ne'er heard out
o' a human thrapple ;—and, unless the deil
wad rise amang them to gie them a lesson,
I thinkna that their talent at cursing could
be amended. The warst o't is, they bid us
aye gang up the loch, and see what we'll
land in."

Adding Andrew's information to what I
had myself observed, I could scarce doubt
that some attack was meditated upon our
party. The road, as we advanced, seemed to afford every facility for such an un-

pleasant interruption. At first it winded
apart fiom the lake through marshy meadow ground, overgrown with copsewood,
now traversing dark and close thickets
which would have admitted an ambuscade
to be sheltered within a few yards of our
line of march, and frequently crossing
rough mountain torrents, some of which
took the soldiers up to the knees, and run
with such violence, that their force could
only be stemmed by the strength of two
or three men holding fast by each others'
arms. It certainly appeared to me, though
altogether unacquainted with military affairs, that a sort of half-savage warriors, as
I had heard the Highlanders asserted to
be, might, in such passes as these, attack a
party of regular forces with great advantage. The Baillie's good sense and shrewd
observation had led him to the same con-
clusion, as I understood from his requesting to speak with the Captain, whom he addressed nearly in the following terms :—
" Captain, it's no to fleech ony favour out

o' ye, for I scorn it—and it's under protest
that I reserve my action and pleas of op-
pression and wrongous imprisonment;—
but, being a friend to King George and his
army, I take the liberty to speer—Dinna
ye think ye might tak a better time to gang
up this glen? If ye are seeking Rob Roy,
he's kenn'd to be better than half a hun-
der men strong when he's at the fewest;
and if he brings in the Glengyle folk, and
the Glenfinlas and Balquidder lads, he may
come to gie you your kail through the
reek; and it's my sincere advice, as a
king's friend, ye had better take back again
to the Clachan, for thae women at Aberfoil are like the scarts and sea-maws at the
Cumries, there's aye foul weather follows
their skirling."

"Make yourself easy, sir," replied Captain Thornton, "I am in the execution of
my orders. And as you say you are a
friend to King George, you will be glad
to learn, that it is impossible that this gang
of ruffians, whose license has disturbed the

country so long, can escape the measures now taken to suppress them. The horse squadron of militia, commanded by Major Galbraith, is already joined by two more troops of cavalry, which will occupy all the lower passes of this wild country ; three hundred Highlanders, under the two gen‑ tlemen you saw at the inn, are in posses‑ sion of the upper part, and various strong parties from the garrison are securing the hills and glens in different directions. Our last accounts of Rob Roy correspond with what this fellow has confessed, that, find‑ ing himself surrounded on all sides, he had dismissed the greater part of his followers, with the purpose either of lying concealed, or of making his escape through his supe‑ rior knowledge of the passes."

" I dinna ken," said the Baillie, " there's mair brandy than brains in Garschatta‑ chin's head this morning—And I wadna, an' I were you, Captain, rest my main dependence on the Hielandmen—hawks winna pike out hawks' een.—They may

quarrel amang themsells, and gie ilk ither
ill names, and maybe a slash wi' a claymore, but they are sure to join in the lang
run against a' civilized folk that wear breeks
on their hinder ends, and hae purses in
their pouches."

Apparently these admonitions were not
altogether thrown away on Captain Thornton. He re-formed his line of march, commanded his soldiers to unsling their firelocks and fix their bayonets, and formed
an advanced and rear-guard, each consist-
ing of a non-commissioned officer and two
soldiers, who received strict orders to keep
an alert look-out. Dougal underwent another and very close examination, in which
he stedfastly asserted the truth of what he
had before affirmed; and being rebuked on
account of the suspicious and dangerous
appearance of the route by which he was
guiding them, he answered with a sort of
testiness that seemed very natural, " Her
nainsell didna mak ta road—an' shentlemans likit grand roads, she suld hae pided
at Glasco."

All this passed off well enough, and we resumed our progress.

' Our route, though leading towards the lake, had hitherto been so much shaded by wood, that we only from time to time obtained a glimpse of that beautiful sheet of water. But the road now suddenly emerged from the forest ground, and, winding close by the margin of the loch, afforded us a full view of its spacious mirror, which now, the breeze having totally subsided, reflected in still magnificence the high dark heathy mountains, huge grey rocks, and shagged banks by which it is encircled. The hills now sunk on its margin so closely, and were so broken and precipitous, as to afford no passage except just upon the narrow line of the track which we occupied, and which was overhung with rocks, from which we might have been destroyed merely by rolling down stones, without much possibility of offering resistance. Add to this, that, as the road winded round every promontory and bay which indented the lake,

there was rarely a possibility of seeing a
hundred yards before us. Our commander
appeared to take some alarm at the nature
of the pass in which he was engaged, which
displayed itself in repeated orders to his
soldiers to be on the alert, and in many
threats of instant death to Dougal, if he
should be found to have led them into
danger. Dougal received these threats
with an air of stupid impenetrability, which
might arise either from conscious inno-
cence, or from dogged resolution.

"If shentlemens were seeking ta Red
Gregarach," he said, " to be sure they
couldna expect to find her without some
wee danger."

Just as the Highlander uttered these
words, a halt was made by the corporal
commanding the advance, who sent back
one of the files who formed it, to tell the
captain that the path in front was occupied by Highlanders, stationed on a commanding point of particular difficulty. Almost at the same instant a soldier from the

rear came to say, that they heard the sound
of a bag-pipe in the woods through which
we had just passed.   Captain Thornton, a
man of conduct as well as courage, instantly
resolved to force the pass in front, without
waiting till he was assailed from the rear ;
and, assuring his soldiers that the bagpipes which they heard were those of the
friendly Highlanders who were advancing
to their assistance, he stated to them the
importance of advancing and securing Rob
Roy, if possible, before these auxiliaries
should come up to divide with them the
honour, as well as the reward which was
placed on the head of this celebrated freebooter.   He therefore ordered the rear-
guard to join the centre, and both to close
up to the advance, doubling his files, so as
to occupy with his column the whole prac-
ticable part of the road, and to present
such a front as its breadth admitted. Dougal, to whom he said in a whisper, " You
dog, if you have deceived me you shall die
for it," was placed in the centre, between

two grenadiers, with positive orders to shoot him, if he attempted an escape. The same situation was assigned to us as being the safest, and Captain Thornton, taking his half-pike from the soldier who carried it, placed himself at the head of his little detachment, and gave the word to march forward.

The party advanced with the firmness of English soldiers; not so Andrew Fair-service, who was frightened out of his wits; and not so, if truth must be told, either the Baillie or I myself, who, without feeling the same degree of trepidation, could not with stoical indifference see our lives exposed to hazard in a quarrel with which we had no concern. But there was neither time for remonstrance nor remedy.

We approached within about twenty yards of the spot where the advanced-guard had seen some appearance of an enemy. It was one of those promontories which run into the lake, and round the

base of which the road had hitherto winded
in the manner I have described. In the
present case, however, the track, instead of
keeping the water's edge, scaled the promontory by one or two rapid zigzags, carried in a broken track along the precipitous
face of a slaty grey rock, which would otherwise have been absolutely inaccessible. On
the top of this rock, only to be approached by a road so broken, so narrow, and so
precarious, the corporal declared he had
seen the bonnets and long-barrelled guns
of several mountaineers, apparently couched among the long heath and brush-wood
which crested the eminence. Captain
Thornton ordered him to move forward
with three files, to dislodge the supposed
ambuscade, while at a more slow but steady
pace, he advanced to his support with the
rest of his party.

  The attack which he meditated was prevented by the unexpected apparition of
a female upon the summit of the rock.
" Stand !" she said, with a commanding

tone, " and tell me what ye seek in Mac-
Gregor's country?"

I have seldom seen a finer or more commanding form than this woman. She might
be between the term of forty and fifty years,
and had a countenance which must once
have been of a masculine cast of beauty;
though now, imprinted with deep lines by
exposure to rough weather, and perhaps
by the wasting influence of grief and passion, it's features were only strong, harsh,
and expressive. She wore her plaid, not
drawn around her head and shoulders, as
is the fashion of the women in Scotland,
but disposed around her body as the Highland soldiers wear their's. She had a man's
bonnet, with a feather in it, an unsheathed
sword in her hand; and a pair of pistols at
her girdle.

" It's Helen Campbell, Rob's wife," said
the Baillie, in a whisper of considerable
alarm; " and there will be broken heads
amang us or it's lang."

" What seek ye here?" she asked again.

at Captain Thornton, who had himself advanced to reconnoitre.

" We seek the outlaw, Rob Roy Mac-Gregor Campbell," answered the officer, " and make no war on women ; therefore offer no vain opposition to the king's troops, and assure yourself of civil treatment."

" Ay," retorted the Amazon, " I am no stranger to your tender mercies. Ye have left me neither name nor fame—my mother's bones will shrink aside in their grave when mine are laid beside them.—Ye have left me and mine neither house nor hold, blanket nor bedding, cattle to feed us, or flocks to clothe us—Ye have taken from us all—all—the very name of our ancestors have ye taken away, and now ye come for our lives."

" I seek no man's life," replied the Captain ; " I only execute my orders. If you are alone, good woman, you have nought 'to fear—if there are any with you so rash as to offer useless resistance, their own blood be on their own heads—Move forward, serjeant."

"Forward—march," said the non-commissioned officer. "Huzza, my boys, for Rob Roy's head or a purse of gold!"

He quickened his pace into a run, followed by the six soldiers; but as they attained the first traverse of the ascent, the flash of a dozen of firelocks from various parts of the pass parted in quick succession and deliberate aim. The serjeant, shot through the body, still struggled to gain the ascent, raised himself by his hands to clamber up the face of the rock, but relaxed his grasp, after a desperate effort, and falling, rolled from the face of the cliff into the deep lake, where he perished. Of the soldiers three fell, slain or disabled; the others retreated on their main body, all more or less wounded.

"Grenadiers, to the front," said Captain Thornton.—You are to recollect, that in these days this description of soldiers actually carried that destructive species of firework from which they derive their name. The four grenadiers moved to the front accordingly. The officer commanded the rest of the party to be ready to support them, and only saying to us, "Look to your safety, gentlemen," gave, in rapid succession, the word to the grenadiers : " Open your pouches—handle your grenades—blow your matches—fall on."

The whole advanced with a shout, headed by Captain Thornton, the grenadiers preparing to throw their grenades among the bushes where the ambuscade lay, and the musketeers to support them by an instant and close assault. Dougal, forgotten in the scuffle, wisely crept into the thicket that overhung that part of the road where we had first halted, which he ascended with the activity of a wild cat. I followed his example instinctively, recollecting that the fire of the Highlanders would sweep the open track. I clambered until out of breath ; for a continued spattering fire, in which every shot was multiplied by a thou-

sand echoes, the hissing of the kindled fu-
sees of the grenades, and the successive
explosion of those missiles, mingled with
the huzzas of the soldiers, and the yells
and cries of their Highland antagonists,
formed a contrast which added—I do not
shame to own it—wings to my desire to
reach a place of safety. The difficulties of
the ascent soon increased so much that I
despaired of reaching Dougal, who seemed to swing himself from rock to rock,
and stump to stump, with the facility of a
squirrel, and I turned down my eyes to see
what had become of my other companions.
Both were brought to a very awkward still-
stand.

The Baillie, to whom I suppose fear
had given a temporary share of agility,
had ascended about twenty feet from the
path, when his foot slipping, as he strad-
dled from one huge fragment of rock to
another, he would have slumbered with
his father the deacon, whose acts and
words he was so fond of quoting, but for

a projecting branch of a ragged thorn, which, catching hold of the skirts of his riding-coat, supported him in mid air, where he dangled not unlike to the sign of the Golden Fleece over the door of a mercer in Ludgate-hill.

As for Andrew Fairservice, he had advanced with better success, until he had attained the top of a bare cliff, which, rising above the wood, exposed him, at least in his own opinion, to all the dangers of the neighbouring skirmish, while, at the same time, it was of such a precipitous and impracticable nature, that he dared neither to advance nor retreat. Footing it up and down upon the narrow space which the top of the cliff afforded, (very like a fellow at a country-fair dancing upon a trencher,) he roared for mercy in Gaelic and English alternately, according to the side on which the scale of victory seemed to predominate, while his exclamations were only answered by the groans of the Baillie, who suffered much, not only from apprehension, but from the pendulous posture in which he hung suspended by the loins.

On perceiving the Baillie's precarious situation, my first idea was to attempt to render him assistance ; but this was impossible without the concurrence of Andrew, whom neither sign, nor entreaty, nor command, nor expostulation, could inspire with courage to adventure the descent from his painful elevation, where, like an unskilful and obnoxious minister of state, unable to escape from the eminence to which he had presumptuously ascended, he continued to pour forth piteous prayers for mercy, which no one heard, and to skip to and fro, writhing his body into all possible antick shapes to avoid the balls which he conceived to be whistling around him.

In a few minutes this cause of terror ceased, for the fire, at first so well sustained, now sunk at once, a sure sign that the conflict was concluded. To gain some spot from which I could see how the day had gone was now my object, in order to appeal to the mercy of the victors, who, I trusted, (whichever side might be gainers,) would not suffer the honest Bailiie to remain suspend- ed, like the coffin of Mahomet, between Heaven and earth, without lending a hand. to disengage him. At length, by dint of scrambling, I found a spot which com- manded a view of the field of battle. It was indeed ended ; and as my mind already augured, from the place and circumstances attending the contest, it had terminated in. the defeat of Captain Thornton. I saw a party of Highlanders in the act of disarm- ing that officer, and the scanty remainder of his party. They consisted of about twelve men, most of whom were wounded, who, surrounded by treble their number, and without the power either to advance or retreat, exposed to a murderous and well-aimed fire, which they had no means of returning with effect, had at length laid down their arms by the orders of their of- ficer, when he saw that the road in his rear was occupied, and that protracted resist-

ance would be only wasting the lives of
his brave followers. By the Highlanders,
who fought under cover, the victory was
cheaply bought, at the expence of one man
slain and two wounded by the grenades.
All this I learned afterwards. At present
I only comprehended the general result of
the day, from seeing the English officer,
whose face was covered with blood, stripped of his hat and arms, and his men, with
sullen and dejected countenances, which
marked their deep regret, enduring, from
the wild and martial figures who surrounded them, the severe measures to which the
laws of war subject the vanquished for security of the victors.

CHAPTER IV.

"Woe to the vanquish'd!" was stern Brenno's word
When sunk proud Rome beneath the Gallic sword—
"Woe to the vanquish'd!" when his massive blade
Bore down the scale against her ransom weigh'd;
And on the field of foughten battle still,
Woe knows no limit save the victor's will.

The Gaulliad.

I ANXIOUSLY endeavoured to distinguish
Dougal among the victors. I had little
doubt that the part he had played was assumed, on purpose to lead the English officer into the defile, and I could not help
admiring the address with which the ignorant, and apparently half-brutal savage, had
veiled his purpose, and the affected reluctance with which he had suffered to be ex-
tracted from him the false information which
it must have been his purpose from the beginning to communicate. I foresaw we
should incur some danger on approaching

'the victors in the first flush of their success, which was not unstained with cruelty, for one or two of the soldiers, whose wounds prevented them from rising, were poniarded by the victors, or rather by some ragged Highland boys who had mingled with them. I concluded, therefore, it would be unsafe to present ourselves without some mediation ; and as Campbell, whom I now could not but identify with the celebrated freebooter Rob Roy, was nowhere to be seen, I resolved to claim the protection of his emissary Dougal.

After gazing everywhere in vain, I at length retraced my steps to see what assistance I could individually render to my unlucky friend, when, to my great joy, I saw Mr Jarvie delivered from his state of suspence ; and though very black in the face, and much deranged in the garments, safely seated beneath the rock, in front of which he had been so lately suspended. I hastened to join him and offer my congratulations, which he was at first far from receiving in the spirit of cordiality with which they were offered. A heavy fit of coughing scarce permitted him breath enough to express the broken hints which he threw out against my sincerity.

" Uh ! uh ! uh ! uh !—they say a friend —uh ! uh !—a friend sticketh closer than a brither—uh ! uh ! uh !—When I came up here, Maister Osbaldistone, to this country, cursed of God and man—uh ! uh !—Heaven forgi'e me for swearing—on nae man's errand but your's, d'ye think it was fair— uh ! uh !—to leave me, first, to be shot or drowned atween red-wud Highlanders and red-coats ; and next, to be hung up between Heaven and earth, like an auld potatoe-bogle, without sae muckle as trying— uh ! uh !—sae muckle as trying to relieve me ?"

I made a thousand apologies, and laboured so hard to represent the impossibility of my affording him relief by my own unassisted exertions, that at length I succeeded, and the Baillie, who was as placa-

ble as hasty in his temper, extended his favour to me once more. I next took the liberty of asking him how he had contrived
to extricate himself.

" Me extricate! I might hae hung there
till the day of judgment, or I could hae
helped mysell, wi' my head hinging doun
on the tae side, and my heels on the tother,
like the yarn-scales in the weigh-house. It
was the creature Dougal that extricated
me, as he did yestreen—he cutted aff the
tails o' my coat wi' his durk, and another
gillie and him set me on my legs as clever-
ly as if I had never been aff them.—But to
see what a thing gude braid claith is—had
I been in ony o' your rotten French cam-
lets now, or your drap-de-berries, it would
hae screeded like an auld rag wi' sic a
weight as mine.—But fair fa' the weaver
that wrought the weft o't—I swung and
bobbit yonder as safe as a gabbart that's
moor'd by a three-plie cable at the Broom-
ielaw."

I now enquired what had become of his
preserver.

" The creature," so he continued to call
the Highlandman, " contrived to let me
ken there wad be danger in gaun near
the leddy till he came back, and bade me
stay here—I am o' the mind," he continued, " that he's seeking after you—it's a
considerate creature — and troth, I wad
swear he was right about the leddy, as he
ca's her, too—Helen Campbell was nane o'
the maist douce maidens nor meekest wives
neither, and folk says that Rob himsell
stands in awe o' her. I doubt she winna
ken me, for it's mony years since we met—
I am clear for waiting for the Dougal creature or we gang near her."

I signified my acquiescence in this reasoning, but it was not the will of fate that
day that the Baillie's prudence should pro-
fit himself or any one else.

Andrew Fairservice, though he had ceased to caper on the pinnacle, upon the ces-
sation of the firing which had given occasion for this whimsical exercise, continued,
as perched on the top of an exposed cliff, too

conspicuous an object to escape the sharp
eyes of the Highlanders, when they had
time to look a little around them. We were
apprized he was discovered, by a wild and
loud halloo set up among the assembled
victors, three or four of whom instantly
plunged into the copsewood, and ascended
the rocky side of the hill in different directions towards the place where they had
discovered this whimsical apparition.

Those who arrived first within gun-shot of
poor Andrew, did not trouble themselves to
offer him any assistance in the ticklish posture of his affairs, but levelling their long
Spanish-barrelled guns, gave him to understand by signs, which admitted of no mis-
construction, that he must contrive to come
down and submit himself to their mercy,
or be marked at from beneath, like a regi-
mental target set up for ball-practice. With
such a formidable hint for venturous exertion, Andrew Fairservice could no longer
hesitate ; the more imminent peril over-

came his sense of that which seemed less
inevitable, and he began to descend the
cliff at all risks, clutching to the ivy and
oak stumps, and projecting fragments of
rock, with an almost feverish anxiety, and
never failing, as circumstances left him a
hand at liberty, to extend it to the plaided
gentry below in an attitude of supplication,
as if to deprecate the discharge of their le-
velled fire-arms.   In a word, the fellow under the influence of a counteracting motive
for terror, achieved a safe descent from his
perilous eminence, which I verily believe
nothing but fear of instant death could
have moved him to attempt.   The awkward mode of Andrew's descent greatly
amused the Highlanders below, who fired
a shot or two while he was engaged in it,
without the purpose of injuring him, as I
believe, but merely to enhance the amuse-
ment they derived from his extreme terror, and the superlative exertions of agility
to which it excited.

At length he attained firm and comparatively level ground, or rather, to speak more correctly, his foot slipping at the last point of descent, he fell on the earth at his full length, and was raised by the assistance of the Highlanders, who stood to receive him, and who, ere he gained his legs, stripped him not only of the whole contents of his pockets, but of periwig, hat, coat, doublet, stockings, and shoes, performing the feat with such admirable celerity, that, although he fell on his back a well-clothed and decent burgher-looking serving-man, he arose a forked, uncased, bald-pated, beggarly-looking, scare-crow. Without respect to the pain which his undefended toes experienced from the sharp encounter of the rocks over which they hurried him, those who had detected Andrew proceeded to drag him downward towards the road through all the intervening obstacles.

In the course of their descent, Mr Jarvie and I became exposed to their lynx-eyed observation, and instantly half a dozen armed Highlanders thronged around

us, with drawn dirks and swords presented
at our faces and throats, and cocked pistols
offered against our bodies.   To have offered resistance would have been madness,
especially as we had no weapons capable
of supporting such a demonstration.   We
therefore submitted to our fate ; and, with
great roughness on the part of those who
assisted at our toilette, were in the act of
being reduced to as unsophisticated a state
(to use King Lear's phrase) as the plume-
less biped Andrew Fairservice, who stood
shivering between fear and cold at a few
yards distance.   Good chance, however,
saved us from this extremity of wretched-
ness ; for just as I had yielded up my cravat, (a smart Steinkirk, by the way, and
richly laced,) and the Baillie had been dis-
robed of the fragments of his riding-coat—
enter Dougal, and the scene was changed.
By a high tone of expostulation, mixed
with oaths and threats, (as far as I could
conjecture the tenor of his language from
the violence of his gestures,) he compell-

ed the plunderers, however reluctant, not only to give up their farther depredations on our property, but to restore the spoil they had already appropriated. He snatched my cravat from the fellow who had seized it, and twisted it (in the zeal of his restitution) around my neck with such suffocating energy, as made me think that he had not only been, during his residence at Glasgow, a substitute of the jailor, but moreover had taken lessons as an apprentice of the hangman. He flung the tattered remnants of Mr Jarvie's coat around his shoulders, and as more Highlanders began to flock up towards us from the high road, he led the way downwards, directing and commanding the others to afford us, but particularly the Baillie, the assistance necessary to our descending with comparative ease and safety. It was, however, in vain that Andrew Fairservice employed his lungs in obsecrating a share of Dougal's protection, or at least his interference, to procure restoration of his shoes.

" Na, na," said Dougal in reply, " she's
na gentle body, I trow; her petters hae
ganged parefoot or she's muckle mista'en."
And, leaving Andrew to follow at his leisure, or rather at such leisure as the surrounding crowd were pleased to indulge
him with, he hurried us down to the path-
way in which the skirmish had been fought,
and hastened to present us as additional
captives to the female leader of his band.

We were dragged before her accordingly, Dougal fighting, struggling, scream-
ing, as if he were the party most apprehen-
sive of hurt, and repulsing, by threats and
efforts, all those who attempted to take
a nearer interest in our capture than he
seemed to do himself. At length we were
placed before the heroine of the day, whose
appearance, as well as those of the savage,
uncouth, yet martial figures who surrounded us, struck me, to own the truth, with
considerable apprehension. I do not know
if Helen MacGregor had taken any actual part in the fray, and indeed I was

afterwards given to apprehend the contrary; but the specks of blood on her brow,
her hands, and naked arms, as well as on
the blade of the sword which she continued
to hold in her hand—her flushed countenance, and the disordered state of the ra-
ven locks which escaped from under the
red bonnet and plume that formed her
head-dress, seemed all to intimate that she
had taken an immediate share in the conflict. Her keen black eyes and features
expressed an imagination inflamed by the
pride of gratified revenge, and the triumph
of victory. Yet there was nothing positively sanguinary, or cruel, in her deportment; and she reminded me, when the
immediate alarm of the interview was over,
of some of the paintings I had seen of the
inspired heroines in the catholic churches
of France. She was not, indeed, sufficient-
ly beautiful for a Judith, nor had she the
inspired expression of features which paint-
ers have given to Deborah, or to the wife of
Heber the Kenite, at whose feet the strong

oppressor of Israel, who dwelled in Haro-
sheth of the Gentiles, bowed down, fell,
and lay a dead man. Nevertheless, the enthusiasm by which she was agitated, gave
her countenance and deportment, wildly
dignified in themselves, an air which made
her approach nearly to the ideas of those
wonderful artists, who gave to the eye the
heroines of Scripture history.

I was uncertain in what terms to accost a
personage so uncommon, when Mr Jarvie,
breaking the ice with a preparatory cough,
for the speed with which he had been
brought into her presence had again impeded his respiration, addressed her as follows:
—" Uh ! uh ! &c. &c. I am very happy to
have this joyful opportunity," (a quaver in
his voice strongly bel'ed the emphasis which
he studiously laid on the word joyful)—
" this *joyful* occasion," he resumed, trying
to give the adjective a more suitable accentuation, " to wish my kinsman Robin's
wife a very good morning—Uh ! uh !—
How's a' wi' ye" (by this time he had talked

himself into his usual jog-trot manner,
which exhibited a mixture of familiarity
and self-importance)—" How's a' wi' ye
this lang time ?—Ye'll hae forgotten me,
Mrs MacGregor Campbell, as your cousin—uh! uh!—if a—but ye'll mind my
father, Deacon Nicol Jarvie, in the Saut-
Market o' Glasgow ?—an honest man he
was, and a sponsible, and respectit you
and yours—Sae, as I said before, I am
right glad to see you, Mrs MacGregor
Campbell, as my kinsman's wife. I wad
crave the liberty of a kinsman to salute
you, but that your gillies keep such a dole-
fu' fast haud o' my arms ; and, to speak
Heaven's truth and a magistrate's, ye wadna be the waur of a cogfu' o' water before
ye welcomed your friends."

There was something in the familiarity
of this introduction which ill suited the
exalted state of temper of the person to
whom it was addressed, then busied with
distributing dooms of death, and warm,
from conquest in a perilous encounter.

" What fellow are you," she said, " that dare to claim kindred with the MacGregor, and neither wear his dress nor speak his language ?—What are you, that have the tongue and the habit of the hound, and yet seek to lay down with the deer ?"

" I dinna ken," said the undaunted Baillie, " if the kindred has ever been weel redd out to you yet, cousin—but it's kenn'd and' can be proved. My mother, Elspeth Macfarlane, was the wife of my father, Deacon Nicol Jarvie—peace be wi' them baith— and Elspeth was the daughter of Parlane' Macfarlane, at the Sheeling o' Loch Sloy. Now, this Parlane Macfarlane, as his surviving daughter, Maggy Macfarlane, alias MacNab, wha married Duncan MacNab o' Stuckavrallachan, can testify, stood as near to your gudeman, Robin MacGregor, as in the fourth degree of kindred, for"—

The virago lopped the genealogical tree, by demanding haughtily, " If a stream of rushing water acknowledged any relation

with the portion withdrawn from it for the
mean domestic uses of those who dwelt on
its banks ?"

" Vera true, kinswoman," said the Baillie ; " but for a' that the burn wad be glad
to hae the mill-dam back again in simmer,
when the chuckie-stanes are white in the
sun. I ken weel aneugh you Hieland folk
haud us Glasgow people light and cheap
for our language and our claes; but every
body speaks their native tongue that they
learned in infancy; and it wad be a daft-like
thing to see me wi' my fat wame in a short
Hieland coat, and my puir short houghs
gartered below the knee, like ane o' your
lang-legged gillies—Mair by token, kinswoman," he continued, in defiance of various intimations by which Dougal seemed
to recommend silence, as well as of the
marks of impatience which the Amazon
evinced at his loquacity, " I wad hae ye
to mind that the king's-errand whiles comes
in the cadger's gate, and that, for as high

as ye may think o' the gudeman, as it's right every wife should honour her husband—there's Scripture warrant for that—yet as high as ye haud him, as I was saying, I hae been serviceable to Rob or now;—forbye a set o' pearlins I sent yoursell when ye was gaun to be married, and when Rob was an honest weel-doing drover, and nane o' this unlawfu' wark, wi' fighting, and flashes, and fluf-gibs, disturbing the king's peace and disarming his soldiers."

He had apparently touched on a key which his kinswoman could not brook. She drew herself up to her full height, and betrayed the acuteness of her feelings by a laugh of mingled scorn and bitterness.

"Yes," she said, "you, and such as you, might claim a relation to us when we stooped to be the paltry wretches fit to exist under your dominion, as your hewers of wood and drawers of water—to find cattle for your banquets, and subjects for your laws to oppress and trample on—But now we

are free—free by the very act which left
us neither house nor hearth, food nor covering—which bereaved me of all—of all—
and makes me groan when I think I must
still cumber the earth for other purposes
than those of vengeance. And I will carry
on the work this day has so well commenced, by a deed that shall break all bands
between MacGregor and the Lowland
churles.—Here—Allan—Dougal—bind these
Sassenachs neck and heel together, and
throw them into the Highland loch to seek
for their Highland kinsfolk."

The Baillie, alarmed at this mandate,
was commencing an expostulation which
probably would have only inflamed the
violent passions of the person whom he
addressed, when Dougal threw himself
between them, and in his own language,
which he-spoke with a fluency and rapidity strongly contrasted by the slow, imperfect, and ideot-like manner in which he
expressed himself in English, poured forth

what I doubt not was a very animated pleading in our behalf.

His mistress replied to him, or rather cut short his harangue, by exclaiming in English, (as if determined to make us taste in anticipation the full bitterness of death,) " Base dog, and son of a dog, do you dispute my commands ?—Should I tell ye to cut out their tongues and put them into each other's throats to try which would there best knap Southron, or to tear out their hearts and put them into each other's breasts to see which would there best plot treason against the MacGregor—and such things have been done of old in the day of revenge, when our fathers had wrongs to redress—Should I command you to do this, would it be your part to dispute my orders ?"

" To be sure, to be sure," he replied, " her pleasure suld be dune—tat's but reason—but an' it were—tat is, an' it could be thought the same to her to coup the ill-faured loon of ta red-coat Captain, and hims

corporal Cramp, and twa three o' the red-
coats into the loch, hersel wad do't wi'
muckle mair great satisfaction than to hurt
ta honest civil shentlemans as were friends
to the Gregarach, and came up on the Chief's
assurance, and no to do no treason, as hersel could testify."

The lady was about to reply, when a few
wild strains of a pibroch were heard advancing up the road from Aberfoil, the same
probably which had reached the ears of
Captain Thornton's rear-guard, and determined him to force his way onward rather
than return to the village, on finding the
pass occupied. The skirmish being of very
short duration, the armed men who followed this martial melody, had not, although
quickening their march when they heard
the firing, been able to arrive in time sufficient to take any share in the rencontre.
The victory, therefore, was complete without them, and they now arrived to share in
the triumph of their countrymen.

There was a marked difference betwixt

the appearance of these new comers and
that of the party by which our escort
had been defeated, and it was greatly in
favour of the former. Among the Highlanders who surrounded the Chieftainess,
if I may presume to call her so without offence to grammar, were men in the
extremity of age, boys scarce able to bear
arms, and even women, all, in short, whom
the last necessity urges to take up arms;
and it added a shade of bitter shame to the
dejection which clouded Thornton's manly
countenance, when he found that the numbers and position of a foe, otherwise so des-
picable, had enabled them to conquer his
brave veterans. But the thirty or forty
Highlanders who now joined the others,
were all men in the prime of youth or
manhood, active clean-made fellows, whose
short hose and belted plaids set out their
sinewy limbs to the best advantage. Their
arms were as superior to those of the first
party as their dress and appearance. The
followers of the female Chief had axes,

scythes, and other antique weapons, in aid
of their guns, and some had only clubs,
daggers, and long knives. But of the second party, most had pistols at the belt,
and almost all had dirks hanging at the
pouches which they wore in front. Each
had a good gun in his hand, and a broad-
sword by his side, besides a stout round
target made of light wood, covered with
leather, and curiously studded with brass,
and having a steel pike screwed into the
centre. These hung at their backs on a
march, or while they were engaged in ex-
changing fire with the enemy, and were
worn on the left arm when they charged
with sword in hand.

But it was easy to see that this chosen
band had not arrived from a victory such
as they found their ill-appointed companions
possessed of. The pibroch sent forth occasionally a few wailing notes, expressive of
a very different sentiment from triumph,
and when they appeared before the wife of
their Chieftain it was in silence, and with

downcast and melancholy looks. They
paused when they approached her, and the
pipes again sent forth the same wild and
melancholy strain.

Helen rushed towards them with a countenance in which anger was mingled with
apprehension. " What means this, Allas-
ter ?" she said to the minstrel. " Why a lament in the moment of victory ?—Robert
—Hamish—Where's the MacGregor ?—
where's your father ?"

Her sons, who led the band, advanced
with slow and irresolute steps towards her,
and murmured a few words in Gaelic, at
hearing which she set up a shriek that
made the rocks ring again, in which all
the women and boys joined, clapping their
hands and yelling, as if their lives had been
expiring in the sound. The mountain
echoes, silent since the military sounds of
battle had ceased, had now to answer these
frantic and discordant shrieks of sorrow,
which drove the very night-birds from their
haunts in the rocks, as if they were startled

to hear orgies more hideous and ill-omened than their own, performed in the face of
open day.

"Taken!" repeated Helen, when the
clamour had subsided — " Taken ! — captive!—and you live to say so ?—Coward
dogs! did I nurse you for this, that you
should spare your blood on your father's
enemies ? or see him prisoner, and come
back to tell it ?"

The sons of MacGregor, to whom this
expostulation was addressed, were youths,
of whom the eldest had hardly attained his
twentieth year. He was called Robert ;
but, to distinguish him from his father, the
Highlanders added the epithet, *Og*, or the
Less. Dark hair, and dark features, with a
ruddy glow of health and animation, and a
form strong and well-set beyond his years,
completed the sketch of the young mountaineer. *Hamish*, or James, was taller by
the head, and much handsomer than his
brother ; his light-blue eyes, with a profusion of fair hair, which streamed from un-

der his smart blue bonnet, made his whole
appearance a most favourable specimen of
the Highland youth.

Both now stood before their mother
with countenances clouded with grief and
shame, and listened, with the most respectful submission, to the reproaches with
which she loaded them. At length, when
her resentment appeared in some degree
to subside, the eldest, speaking in English,
probably that he might not be understood
by their followers, endeavoured respect-
fully to vindicate himself and his brother
from his mother's reproaches. I was so
near him as to comprehend much of what
he said; and, as it was of much consequence to me to be possessed of information in this strange crisis, I failed not to
listen as attentively as I could.

"The MacGregor," his son stated, "had
been called out upon a trysting with a
Lowland hallion, who came with a token
from"—he muttered the name very low,
but I thought it sounded like my own.—

" The MacGregor," he said, " accepted of
the invitation, but commanded the Saxon
who brought the message to be detained as
a hostage, that good faith should be observed to him. Accordingly he went to
the place of appointment,' (which had
some wild Highland name that I cannot
remember,) " attended only by Angus
Breck and little Rory, commanding no one
to follow him ; within half an hour Angus
Breck came back with the doleful tidings
that the MacGregor had been surprised
and made prisoner by a party of Lennox
militia, under Galbraith of Garschattachin."
He added, " that Galbraith, on being threatened by MacGregor, who, upon his capture, menaced him with retaliation on the
person of the hostage, had treated the
threat with great contempt, replying, ' Let
every one hang his man ; we'll hang the
thief, and your catherans may hang the
gauger, Rob, and the country will be rid
of two damned things at once, a wild
Highlander and a revenue officer.' Angus

1

Breck, less carefully looked to than his master, contrived to escape from the hands of the captors, after having been in their custody long enough to hear this discussion and to bring off the news."

" And did you learn this, you false-hearted traitor," said the wife of MacGregor, " and not instantly rush to your father's rescue to bring him off, or leave your body on the place ?"

The young MacGregor modestly replied, by representing the very superior force of the enemy, and stated, that as they made no preparation for leaving the country, he had fallen back up the glen with the purpose of collecting a band sufficient to attempt a rescue with some tolerable chance of success. At length he said, " The militiamen would quarter, he understood, in the neighbouring house of Gartartan, or the old castle in the port of Monteith, or some other strong-hold, which, although strong and defensible, was nevertheless capable of being surprised, could they but

get enough of men assembled for the purpose."

I understood afterwards that the rest of
the freebooter's followers were divided into two strong bands, one destined to watch
the remaining garrison of Inversnaid, a
party of which, under Captain Thornton,
had been defeated; and another to shew
front to the Highland clans who had united with the regular troops and Lowlanders in this hostile and combined inva-
sion of that mountainous and desolate ter-
ritory, which, lying between the lakes of
Loch-Lomond, Loch-Katrine, and Loch-
Hard, was at this time currently called
Rob Roy's country. Messengers were dispatched in great haste, to concentrate, as
I supposed, their forces, with a view to the
purposed attack on the Lowlanders; and
the dejection and despair, at first visible
on each countenance, gave place to the
hope of rescuing their leader, and to the
thirst of vengeance. It was under the
burning influence of the latter passion that

the wife of MacGregor commanded that
the hostage exchanged for his safety should
be brought into her presence. I believe
her sons had kept this unfortunate wretch
out of her sight, for fear of the consequences; but if it was so, their humane
precaution only postponed his fate. They
dragged forward at her summons a wretch
already half dead with terror, in whose
agonized features I recognized, to my horror and astonishment, my old acquaintance
Morris.

He fell prostrate before the female Chief
with an effort to clasp her knees, from
which she drew back, as if his touch had
been pollution, so that all he could do in
token of the extremity of his humiliation,
was to kiss the hem of her plaid. I never
heard entreaties for life poured forth with
such agony of spirit. The ecstacy of fear
was such, that, instead of paralyzing his
tongue, as on ordinary occasions, it even
rendered him eloquent, and, with cheeks
pale as ashes, hands compressed in agony,

eyes that seemed to be taking their last look of all mortal objects, he protested, with the deepest oaths, his total ignorance of any design on the person of Rob Roy, whom he swore he loved and honoured as his own soul.—In the inconsistency of his terror, he said, he was but the agent of others, and he muttered the name of Rashleigh.—He prayed but for life—for life he would give all he had in the world ;—it was but life he asked—life, if it were to be prolonged under tortures and privations ;—he asked only breath, though it should be drawn in the damps of the lowest caverns of their hills.

It is impossible to describe the scorn, the loathing and contempt, with which the wife of MacGregor regarded this wretched petitioner for the poor boon of existence.

" I could have bid you live," she said, " had life been to you the same weary and wasting burthen that it is to me—that it is to every noble and generous mind.—But

you—wretch! you could creep through the
world unaffected by its various disgraces,
its ineffable miseries, its constantly accu-
mulating masses of crime and sorrow,—
you could live and enjoy yourself, while
the noble-minded are betrayed, —while
nameless and birthless villains tread on
the neck of the brave and the long-de-
scended,—you could enjoy yourself, like a
butcher's dog in the shambles, battoning
on garbage, while the slaughter of the brave
went on around you! This enjoyment you
shall not live to partake of; you shall die,
base dog, and that before yon cloud has
passed over the sun."

She gave a brief command in Gaelic to
her attendants, two of whom seized upon
the prostrate suppliant, and hurried him to
the brink of a cliff which overhung the
flood. He set up the most piercing and
dreadful cries that fear ever uttered—I
may well term them dreadful, for they
haunted my sleep for years afterward. As
the murderers, or executioners, call them as

you will, dragged him along, he recognized
me even in that moment of horror, and exclaimed, in the last articulate words I ever
heard him utter, " O, Mr Osbaldistone,
save me !—save me !"

‹ I was so much moved by this horrid
spectacle, that, although in momentary ex-
pectation of sharing his fate, I did attempt
to speak in his behalf, but, as might have
been expected, my interference was sternly
disregarded. The victim was held fast by
some, while others, binding a large heavy
stone in a plaid, tied it round his neck, and
others again eagerly stripped him of some
part of his dress. Half-naked, and thus
manacled, they hurled him into the lake,
there about twelve feet deep, drowning
his last death-shriek with a loud halloo of
vindictive triumph, above which, however,
the yell of mortal agony was distinctly
heard. The heavy burden splashed in the
dark-blue waters of the lake, and the Highlanders, with their pole-axes and swords,
watched an instant, to guard, lest, extri-

cating himself from the load to which he was attached, he might have struggled to regain the shore. But the knot had been securely bound; the victim sunk without effort; the waters, which his fall had disturbed, settled calmly over him, and the unit of that life for which he had pleaded so strongly, was for ever withdrawn from the sum of human existence.

CHAPTER V.

And be he safe restored ere evening set,
Or if there's vengeance in an injured heart,
And power to wreak it in an armed hand,
Your land shall ache for't.

Old Play.

I KNOW not why it is, that a single deed
of violence and cruelty affects our nerves
more than when these are exercised on a
more extended scale. I had seen that day
several of my brave countrymen fall in
battle—it seemed to me that they met a
lot appropriate to humanity ; and my bosom, though thrilling with interest, was
affected with nothing of that sickening horror with which I beheld the unfortunate
Morris put to death without resistance,
and in cold blood. I looked at my companion, Mr Jarvie, whose face reflected the
feelings which were painted in mine. In-

deed, he could not so suppress his horror,
but that the words escaped him in a low
and broken whisper,——

"I take up my protest against this deed,
as a bloody and cruel murder—it is a cursed deed, and God will avenge it in his due
way and time."

"Then you do not fear to follow?" said
the virago, bending on him a look of death,
such as that with which a hawk looks at his
prey ere he pounces.

"Kinswoman," said the Baillie, "nae
man willingly wad cut short his thread of
life before the end o' his pirn was fairly
measured off on the yarn-winles.—And I
hae muckle to do, an I be spared, in this
warld—public and private business, as weel
that belanging to the magistracy as to my
ain particular—and nae doubt I hae some
to depend on me, as puir Mattie, wha is an
orphan—She's a far-awa' cousin o' the Laird
o' Limmerfield—sae that, laying a' this thegither—skin for skin, yea, all that a man
hath will he give for his life."

" And were I to set you at liberty, what name would you give to the drowning of that Saxon dog ?"

" Uh ! uh !—hem ! hem !" said the Baillie, clearing his throat as well as he could, " I suld study to say as little on that score as might be—least said is sunest mended."

" But if you were called on by the courts, as you term them, of justice, what then would be your answer ?"

The Baillie looked this way and that way, like one who meditates an escape, and then answered in the tone of one, who, seeing no means of accomplishing a retreat, determines to stand the brunt of battle.—" I see what you are driving me to the wa' about. But I'll tell you't plain, kinswoman, I behooved just to speak according to my ain conscience ; and though your ain gudeman, that I wish had been here for his ain sake and mine, as weel as the puir Hieland creature Dougal, can tell ye that Nicol Jarvie can wink as hard at a friend's failings as ony body, yet

I'se tell ye, kinswoman, mine's ne'er be
the tongue to belie my thought ; and
sooner than say that yonder puir wretch
was lawfully slaughtered, I wad consent to
be laid beside him—though I think ye are
the first Hieland woman wad mint sic a
doom to her husband's kinsman but four
times removed."

It is probable that the tone of firmness
assumed by the Baillie in his last speech
was better suited to make an impression
on the hard heart of his kinswoman than
the tone of supplication he had hitherto
assumed, as gems can be cut with steel,
though they resist softer metals. She commanded us both to be placed before her.
" Your name," she said to me; " is Osbaldistone ?—the dead dog, whose death you
have witnessed, called you so."

" My name *is* Osbaldistone," was my
answer.

" Rashleigh then, I suppose, is your
Christian name ?" she pursued.

" No ; my name is Francis."

" But you know Rashleigh Osbaldistone ?—He is your brother, if I mistake
not, at least your kinsman and near
friend."

" He is my kinsman," I replied, " and
not my friend. We were lately engaged
together in a rencontre, when we were separated by a person whom I understand to
be your husband. My blood is hardly yet
dried on his sword, and the wound on my
side is yet green. I have little reason to
acknowledge him as a friend."

" Then," she replied, " if a stranger to
his intrigues, you can go in safety to Garschattachin and his party without fear of
being detained, and carry them a message
from the wife of the MacGregor ?"

I answered, " That I knew no reasonable cause why the militia gentlemen should
detain me ; that I had no reason, on my
own account, to fear being in their hands ;
and that if my going on her embassy would
act as a protection to my friend and servant, who were her prisoners, I was ready

to set out directly. I took the opportunity to say, " That I had come into this country on her husband's invitation, and his assurance that he would aid me in some important matters in which I was interested ;
that my companion, Mr Jarvie, had accompanied me on the same errand."

" And I wish Mr Jarvie's boots had
been fu' o' boiling water when he drew
them on for sic a purpose," interrupted the
Baillie.

" You may read your father," said Helen
MacGregor, turning to her sons, " in what
this young Saxon tells us—Wise only when
the bonnet is on his head, and the sword is
in his hand, he never exchanges the tartan
for the broad cloth, but he runs himself
into the miserable intrigues of the Lowlands, and becomes again, after all he has
suffered, their agent — their tool — their
slave."

" Add, madam," said I, " and their benefactor."

" Be it so," she said ; " for it is the

most empty title of them all, since he has
uniformly sown benefits to reap a harvest
of the most foul ingratitude.—But enough
of this—I shall cause you to be guided to
the enemy's outposts—ask for their commander, and deliver him this message from
me, Helen MacGregor, that if they injure
a hair of MacGregor's head, and if they do
not set him at liberty within the space of
twelve hours, there is not a lady in the
Lennox but shall before Christmas cry the
coronach for them she will be loth to lose,
—there is not a farmer but shall sing well-
a-wa over a burnt barnyard and an empty
byre,—there is not a laird nor heritor shall
lay his head on the pillow at night with the
assurance of being a live man in the morning,—and, to begin as we are to end, so
soon as the term is expired, I will send them
this Glasgow Baillie, and this Saxon Captain, and all the rest of my prisoners, each
bundled in a plaid, and chopped into as
many pieces as there are checks in the
tartan."

As she paused in her denunciation, Captain Thornton, who was within hearing,
added with great coolness, " Present my
compliments—Captain Thornton's, of the
Royals, compliments—to the commanding
officer, and tell him to do his duty and secure his prisoner, and not waste a thought
upon me. If I have been fool enough to
have been led into an ambuscade by these
artful savages, I am wise enough to know
how to die for it without disgracing the
service. I am only sorry for my poor fellows," he said, " that have fallen into such
butcherly hands."

" Whisht! whisht!" exclaimed the Baillie; " are ye weary o' your life ?—Ye'll gie
my service to the commanding officer—
Baillie Nicol Jarvie's service—a magistrate
o' Glasgow, as his father the deacon was before him—and tell him, here are a wheen honest men in great trouble, and like to come
to mair ; and the best thing he can do for
the common good, will be just to let Rob
come his wa's up the glen, and nae mair

about it—There's been some ill dune here
already; but as it has lighted chiefly on the
gauger, it winna be muckle worth making
a stir about."

With these very opposite injunctions from
the parties chiefly interested in the success
of my embassy, and with the reiterated
charge of the wife of MacGregor, to remember and detail every word of her injunctions, I was at length suffered to depart; and Andrew Fairservice, chiefly, I
believe, to get rid of his clamorous sup-
plications, was permitted to attend me.
Doubtful, however, that I might use my
horse as a means of escape from my guides,
or desirous to retain a prize of some value, I was given to understand that I was
to perform my journey on foot, escorted
by Hamish MacGregor, the younger brother, who, with two followers, attended, as
well to shew me the way as to reconnoitre
the strength and position of the enemy.
Dougal was ordered on this party, but he
contrived to elude the service, with the

purpose, as we afterwards understood, of watching over Mr Jarvie, whom, according to his wild principles of fidelity, he considered as entitled to his good offices, from having once acted in some measure as his patron or master.

After walking with great rapidity about an hour, we arrived at an eminence covered with brushwood, which gave us a commanding prospect down the valley, and a full view of the post which the militia occupied. Being chiefly cavalry, they had judiciously avoided any attempt to penetrate the pass which had been so unsuccessfully essayed by Captain Thornton. They had taken up their situation with some military skill, on a rising ground, in the centre of the little valley of Aberfoil, through which the river Forth winds its earliest course, and which is formed by two ridges of hills, faced with barricades of limestone rock, intermixed with huge masses of Brescia, or pebbles imbedded in some softer substance which has hardened around,

them like mortar ; and surrounded by the
more lofty mountains in the distance. These
ridges, however, left the valley of breadth
enough to secure the cavalry from any sudden surprise by the mountaineers, and they
had stationed centinels and outposts at proper distances from this main body, in every
direction, so that they might secure full
time to mount and get under arms upon
the least alarm. It was not indeed expected at that time, that Highlanders would
attack cavalry in an open plain, though late
events have shewn that they may do so
with success. When I first knew the Highlanders, they had almost a superstitious
dread of a mounted trooper, the horse being so much more fierce and imposing in
his appearance than the little *shelties* of
their own hills, and being moreover trained, as the more ignorant mountaineers believed, to fight with his feet and his teeth.

.The appearance of the piquetted horses,
feeding in this little vale ; the forms of
the soldiers as they sate, stood, or walk-

ed, in various groups in the vicinity of the
beautiful little river, and of the bare and
romantic rocks' which hedge in the land-
scape on either side, formed a beautiful
foreground, while far to the eastward the
eye caught a glance of the lake of Men-
teith, and Stirling Castle, dimly seen along
with the blue and distant line of the Ochill
Mountains, closed the scene.

After gazing on this scene with great
earnestness, young MacGregor intimated
to me that I was to descend to the station
of the militia and execute my errand to
their commander, enjoining me at the same
time, with a menacing gesture, neither to
inform them who had guided me to that
place, nor where I had parted from my
escort. Thus tutored, I descended towards
the military post, followed by Andrew, who,
only retaining his breeches and stockings
of the English costume, without a hat, bare-
legged, with brogues on his feet, which
Dougal had given him out of compassion,
and having a tattered plaid to supply the

want of all upper garments, looked as if
he had been playing the part of a Highland
Tom-of-Bedlam. We had not proceeded
far before we became visible to one of the
videttes, who, riding towards us, presented
his carabine and commanded me to stand.
I obeyed, and when the soldier came up to
me, I desired to be conducted to his commanding officer. I was immediately brought
where a circle of officers, sitting upon the
grass, seemed in attendance upon one of
superior rank. He wore a cuirass of po-
lished steel, over which were drawn the in-
signia of the ancient Order of the Thistle.
My friend Garschattachin, and many other
gentlemen, some in uniform, others in their
ordinary dress, but all armed and well attended, seemed to receive their orders from
this person of distinction. Many servants
in rich liveries, apparently a part of his
household, were also in attendance.

Having paid to this nobleman the respect which his rank seemed to demand, I
acquainted him that I had been an involun-

tary witness to the king's soldiers having
suffered a defeat from the Highlanders at
the pass of Loch-Ard, (such I had learned
was the name of the place where Mr
Thornton was made prisoner,) and that
the victors threatened every species of extremity to those who had fallen into their
power, as well as to the low country in
general, unless their Chief, who had that
morning been made prisoner, were returned to them uninjured. The Duke (for he
whom I addressed was of no lower rank)
listened to me with great composure, and
then replied, " That he should be ex-
tremely sorry to expose the unfortunate
gentlemen who had been made prisoners
to the cruelty of the barbarians into whose
hands they had fallen, but that it was folly
to suppose that he would deliver up the
very author of all these disorders and of-
fences, and so encourage his followers in
their license. You may return to those
who sent you, and inform them, that I
shall certainly cause Rob Roy Campbell,

whom they call MacGregor, to be executed by break of day, as an outlaw taken
in arms, and deserving death by a thousand acts of violence; that I should be
most justly held unworthy of my situation
and commission did I act otherwise; that
I shall know how to protect the country
against their insolent threats of violence;
and that if they injure a hair of the head
of any of the unfortunate gentlemen whom
an unfortunate accident has thrown into
their power, I will take such ample vengeance—that the very stones of their glens
shall sing woe for it this hundred years to
come!"

I humbly begged leave to remonstrate
respecting the honourable mission imposed
on me, and touched upon the obvious danger attending it, when the noble commander replied, " that such being the case, I
might send my servant."

" The deil be in my feet," said Andrew,
without either having respect to the presence in which he stood, or waiting till I

replied—" the deil be in my feet, if I gang
my tae's length. Do the folk think I hae
another thrapple in my pouch after John
Hielandman's sneckit this ane wi' his jocta-
leg? or that I can dive doun at the tae side
of a Highland loch and rise at the tother,
like a skell-drake?—Na, na—ilk ane for
himsel, and God for us a'. Folk may just
mak a page o' their ain age, and serve
themsells till their bairns grow up, and
gang their ain errands, for Andrew. Rob
Roy never came near the parish of Dreep-
daily to steal either pippin or pear frae me
or mine."

Silencing my follower with some difficulty, I represented to the Duke the great
danger Captain Thornton and Mr Jarvie
would certainly be exposed to, and entreated he might make me the bearer of such
modified terms as might be the means of
saving their lives. I assured him I should
decline no danger if I could be of service;
but from what I had heard and seen, I had
little doubt they would be instantly mur-

dered should the chief of the outlaws suffer death.

The Duke was obviously much affected. " It was a hard case," he said, " and he felt it as such ; but he had a paramount duty to perform to the country—Rob Roy must die !"

I own it was not without emotion that I heard this threat of instant death to my acquaintance Campbell, who had so often testified his good-will towards me. Nor was I singular in the feeling, for many of those around the Duke ventured to express themselves in his favour. " It would be more advisable," they said, " to send him to Stirling Castle, and there detain him a close prisoner, as a pledge for the submission and dispersion of his gang. It were a great pity to expose the country to be plundered, which, now that the long nights approached, it would be found very difficult to prevent, since it was impossible to guard every point, and the Highlanders were sure to select those that were left

exposed." They added, " that there was
great hardship in exposing the unfortunate
prisoners to the almost certain doom of
massacre denounced against them, which
no one doubted would be executed in the
first burst of revenge."

Garschattachin ventured yet further, con-
fiding in the honour of the nobleman whom
he addressed, although he knew he had particular reasons for disliking their prisoner.
" Rob Roy," he said, " though a kittle
neighbour to the low country, and particularly obnoxious to his Grace, and though
he maybe carried the catheran trade farther
than ony man o' his day, was an auld-far-
rand carle, and there might be some means
found of making him hear reason ; whereas
his wife and sons were reckless fiends, without either fear or mercy about them, and,
at the head of a' his limmer louns, would
be a worse plague to the country than ever
he had been." ·

" Pooh ! pooh !" replied his Grace, " it
is the very sense and cunning of this fellow

which has so long maintained his reign—a mere Highland robber would have been put down in as many weeks as he has flourished years. His gang without him is no more to be dreaded as a permanent annoyance—it will no longer exist than a wasp without it's head, which may sting once perhaps, but is instantly crushed into annihilation."

Garschattachin was not so easily silenced.

" I am sure, my Lord Duke," he replied, " I have no favour for Rob, and he as little for me, seeing he has twice cleaned out my ain byres, besides skaith amang my tenants ; but, however"——

" But, however, Garschattachin," said the Duke, with a smile of peculiar expression, " I fancy you think such a freedom may be pardoned in a friend's friend, and Rob's supposed to be no enemy to Major Galbraith's friends over the water."

" If it be so, my Lord," said Garschattachin, in the same tone of jocularity, " it's no the warst thing I have heard of him. But

I wish we heard some news from the clans,
that we have waited for sae lang. I vow
to God they'll keep a Hielandman's word
wi' us—I never kenn'd them better—it's
ill drawing boots upon trews."

"I cannot believe it," said the Duke;
"these gentlemen are known to be men
of honour, and I must necessarily suppose
they are to keep their appointment. Send
out two more horsemen to look for our
friends. We cannot, till their arrival, pretend to attack the pass where Captain
Thornton has suffered himself to be surprised, and which, to my knowledge, ten
men on foot might make good against a
regiment of the best horse in Europe—
Meanwhile let refreshments be given to
the men."

I had the benefit of this last order, the
more necessary and acceptable, as I had
tasted nothing since our hasty meal at
Aberfoil the evening before. The videttes who had been dispatched, returned
without tidings of the expected auxiliaries,

and sunset was approaching, when a Highlander belonging to the clans whose co-
operation was expected, appeared as the
bearer of a letter, which he delivered to the
Duke with a most profound congé.

"Now will I wad a hogshead of claret,"
said Garschattachin, " that this is a message to tell us that these cursed Highland-
men, whom we have fetched here at the ex-
pense of so much plague and vexation, are
going to draw off, and leave us to do our
own business if we can."

" It is even so, gentlemen," said the
Duke, reddening with indignation, after
having perused the letter, which was written upon a very dirty scrap of paper, but
most punctiliously addressed, " For the
much-honoured hands of Ane High and
Mighty Prince, the Duke, &c. &c. &c."
" Our allies," continued the Duke, " have
deserted us, gentlemen, and have made a
separate peace with the enemy."

" It's just the fate of all alliances," said

Garschattachin ; " the Dutch were gaun to
serve us'the same gate, if we had not got
'the start of them at Utrecht."

" You are facetious, sir," said the Duke,
with a frown which shewed how little he
liked the pleasantry, " and our business is
rather of a grave cast just now.—I suppose
no gentleman would advise our attempting
to penetrate farther into the country, unsupported either by friendly Highlanders,
or by infantry from Inversnaid ?"

A general answer announced that the
attempt would be perfect madness.

" Nor would there be great wisdom,"
the Duke added, " in remaining exposed
to a night attack in this place. I therefore
propose that we should retreat to the house
of Duchray and that of Gartartan, and
keep safe and sure watch and ward until
morning. But before we separate, I will
examine Rob Roy before you all, and make
you sensible, by your own eyes and ears, of
the extreme unfitness of leaving him space

for further outrage." He gave orders accordingly, and the prisoner was brought
before him, his arms belted down above
the elbow, and secured to his body by a
horse-girth buckled tight behind him. Two
non-commissioned officers had hold of him,
one on each side, and two file of men with
carabines and fixed bayonets attended for
additional security.

I had never seen this man in the dress
of his country, which set in a striking
point of view the peculiarities of his form.
A shock-head of red hair, which the hat
and periwig of the Lowland costume had
in a great measure concealed, was seen
beneath the Highland bonnet, and verified
the epithet of *Roy*, or Red, by which he
was much better known in the low country than by any other, and is still, I suppose, best remembered. The justice of the
appellation was also vindicated by the appearance of that part of his limbs, from the
bottom of his kilt to the top of his short
hose, which the fashion of his country

dress left bare, and which was covered
with a fell of thick, short, red hair, especially around his knees, which resembled
in this respect, as well as from their sinewy
appearance of extreme strength, the limbs
of a red-coloured Highland bull. Upon
the whole, betwixt the effect produced by
the change of dress, and by my having become acquainted with his real and formidable character, his appearance had acquired
to my eyes something so much wilder and
more striking than it before presented, that
I could scarce recognise him to be the
same person.

His manner was bold, unconstrained
unless by the actual bonds, haughty, and
even dignified. He bowed to the Duke,
nodded to Garschattachin and others, and
shewed some surprise at seeing me among
the party.

" It is long since we have met, Mr
Campbell," said the Duke.

" It is so, my Lord Duke ; I could
have wished it had been," (looking at the

fastening on his arms,) " when I could have better paid the compliments I owe to your Grace—but there's a guid time coming."

" No time like the time present, Mr Campbell," answered the Duke, " for the hours are fast flying that must settle your last account with all mortal affairs. I do not say this to insult your distress, but you must be aware yourself that you draw near the end of your career. I do not deny that you may sometimes have done less harm than others of your unhappy trade, and that you may occasionlly have exhibited marks of talent, and even of a disposition which promised better things. But you are aware how long you have been the terror and the oppressor of a peaceful neighbourhood, and by what acts of violence you have maintained and extended your usurped authority. You know, in short, that you have deserved death, and that you must prepare for it."

· " My Lord," said Rob Roy, " although I may well lay my misfortunes to your Grace's

door, yet I will never say that you yourself
have been the wilful and witling author of
them. My Lord, if I had thought sae, your
Grace would not this day have been sitting in judgment on me ; for you have been
three times within good rifle distance of me
when you were thinking but of the red deer,
and few people have kenn'd me miss my
aim. But as for them that have abused your
Grace's ear, and set you up against a man
that was ance as peacefu' a man as ony in
the land, and made your name the warrant
for driving me to utter extremity,—I have
had some amends of them, and for a' that
your Grace now says, I expect to live to
hae mair."

"I know," said the Duke, in rising anger, " that you are a determined and im-
pudent villain, who will keep his oath if
he swears to mischief; but it shall be my
care to prevent you. You have no enemies
but your own wicked actions."

" Had I called myself Grahame, instead

of Campbell, I might have heard less about them," answered Rob Roy, with dogged resolution.

"You will do well, sir," said the Duke, "to warn your wife and family and followers, to beware how they use the gentlemen now in their hands, as I will requite tenfold on them and their kin and allies the slightest injury done to any of his majesty's liege subjects."

"My Lord," said Roy in answer, "none of my enemies will allege that I have been a blood-thirsty man, and were I now wi' my folk, I could rule four or five hundred wild Hielanders as easy as your Grace those eight or ten lackies and foot-boys. But if your Grace is bent to take the head away from a house, ye may lay your account there will be misrule amang the members. —However, come o't what like, there's an honest man, a kinsman o' my ain, maun come by nae skaith.—Is there ony body here wad do a gude deed for MacGregor —he may repay it, though his hands be now tied."

The Highlander who had delivered the letter to the Duke replied, " I'll do your will for you, MacGregor ; and I'll gang back up the glen on purpose."

He advanced, and received from the prisoner a message to his wife, which, being in Gaelic, I did not understand, but I had little doubt it related to some measures to be taken for the safety of Mr Jarvie.

" Do you hear the fellow's impudence?" said the Duke ; " he confides in his character of a messenger. His conduct is of a piece with his masters', who invited us to make common cause against these freebooters, and have deserted us so soon as they have agreed to surrender the Balquidder lands they were squabbling about.

> " No truth in plaids, no faith in tartan trews,
> Camelion-like, they change a thousand hues."

" Your great ancestor never said so, my Lord," answered Major Galbraith ; " and, with submission, neither would your Grace have occasion to say it, wad ye but be for beginning justice at the well-head—Gie the honest man his mear again—Let every head wear its ain bannet, and the distractions o' the Lennox wad be mended wi' them o' the land."

- "Hush! hush! Garschattachin," said the Duke; "this is language dangerous for you to talk to any one, especially to me; but I presume you reckon yourself a privileged person. Please to draw off your party towards- Gartartan; I shall myself see the prisoner escorted to Duchray, and send you orders to-morrow. You will please grant no leave of absence to any of your troopers."

"Here's auld ordering and counter-ordering," muttered Garschattachin between his teeth. "But patience! patience!—we may ae day play at Change seats, the king's coming."

The two troops of cavalry now formed, and prepared to march off the ground, that they might avail themselves of the remain-

der of daylight to get to their evening quarters. I received an intimation, rather than an
invitation, to attend the party ; and I per-
ceived, that, though no longer considered
as a prisoner, I was yet under some sort of
suspicion.   The times were indeed so dangerous,—the great party questions of Jacobite and Hanoverian divided the country
so effectually,—and the constant disputes
and jealousies between the Highlanders
and Lowlanders, besides a number of in-
explicable causes of feud which separated
the great leading families in Scotland from
each other, occasioned such general suspicion, that a solitary and unprotected stranger was almost sure to meet with something disagreeable in the course of his tra-
vels.   I acquiesced, however, in my destination with the best grace I could, con-
soling myself with the hope that I might
obtain from the captive freebooter some
information concerning Rashleigh and his
machinations. I should do myself injustice
did I not add, that my views were not mere-

ly selfish. I was too much interested in my singular acquaintance not to be desirous of rendering him such services as his unfortunate situation might demand, or admit of his receiving.

CHAPTER VII.

And when he came to broken brigg,
  He bent his bow and swam ;
And when he came to grass growing,
  Set down his feet and ran.

            Gil Morrice.

THE echoes of the rocks and ravines, on
either side of the valley, now rang to the
trumpets of the cavalry, which, forming
themselves into two distinct bodies, began
to move down the valley at a slow trot. That
commanded by Major Galbraith soon took
to the right-hand, and crossed the Forth,
for the purpose of taking up the quarters
assigned them for the night, when they
were to occupy, as I understood, an old
castle in the vicinity. They formed a lively object while crossing the stream, but
were soon lost in winding up the bank on

the opposite side, which was clothed with wood.

We continued our march with considerable good order. To ensure the safe custody of the prisoner, the Duke had caused him to be placed on horseback behind one of his retainers, called, as I was informed, Ewan of Brigglands, one of the largest and strongest men who were present. A horse-belt passed round the bodies of both, and buckled before the yeoman's breast, rendered it impossible for Rob Roy to free himself from his keeper. I was directed to keep close beside them, and accommodated for the purpose with a troop-horse. We were as closely surrounded by the soldiers as the width of the road would permit, and had always at least one, if not two, on each side with pistol in hand. Andrew Fairservice, furnished with a Highland poney of which they had made prey some where or other, was permitted to ride among the other domestics, of whom a great number attended the line of march, though with-

out falling into the ranks of the more regularly trained troopers.

In this manner we travelled for a cer,
tain distance, until we arrived at a place
where we also were to cross the river. The
Forth, as being the outlet of a lake, is of
a considerable depth, even where less important in point of width; and the descent
to the ford was by a broken precipitous
ravine, which only permitted one horseman to descend at once. The rear and
centre of our small body halting on the
bank while the front files passed down in
succession, occasioned a considerable delay, as is usual in such occasions, and even
some confusion; for a number of those
riders, who made no proper part of the
squadron, crowded to the ford without regularity, and made the militia cavalry, although tolerably well drilled, partake in
some degree of their own disorder.

It was while we were thus huddled together on the bank that I heard Rob Roy
whisper to the man behind whom he was

placed on horseback, " Your father, Ewan, wadna hae carried an auld friend to the shambles, like a calf, for a' the Dukes in Christendom."

Ewan returned no answer, but shrugged as one who would express by that sign that what he was doing was none of his own choice.

" And when the MacGregors come down the glen, and ye see toom faulds, a bluidy hearth-stane, and the fire flashing out between the rafters o' your house, ye may be thinking then, Ewan, that were your friend Rob to the fore, you would have had that safe which it will make your heart sair to lose."

Ewan of Brigglands again shrugged and groaned, but remained silent.

" It's a sair thing," continued Rob, sliding his insinuations so gently into Ewan's ear that they reached no other but mine, who certainly saw myself in no shape called upon to destroy his prospects of escape— " It's a sair thing, that Ewan of Brigglands, whom Roy MacGregor has helped with hand, sword, and purse, suld mind a gloom from a great man mair than a friend's life."

Ewan seemed sorely agitated, but was silent. We heard the Duke's voice from the opposite bank call, " Bring over the prisoner."

Ewan put his horse in motion, and just as I heard Roy say, " Never weigh a MacGregor's bluid against a broken whang o' leather, for there will be another accounting to gie for it baith here and hereafter," they passed me hastily, and, dashing forward rather precipitately, entered the water.

" Not yet, sir—not yet," said some of the troopers to me, as I was about to follow, while others pressed forward into the stream.

I saw the Duke on the other side, by the waning light, engaged in commanding his people to get into order, as they landed dispersedly, some higher, some lower. Many had crossed, some were in the water, and the

rest were preparing to follow, when a sudden splash warned me that MacGregor's eloquence had prevailed on Ewan to give him
freedom and a chance for life. The Duke
also heard the sound, and instantly guessed
its meaning. " Dog !" he exclaimed to Ewan
as he landed, " where is your prisoner ?"
and, without waiting to hear the apology
which the terrified vassal began to faulter
forth, he fired a pistol at his head, whether
fatally I know not, and exclaimed, " Gentlemen, disperse and pursue the villain—
An hundred guineas for him that secures
Rob Roy !"

All became an instant scene of the most
lively confusion. Rob Roy, disengaged
from his bonds, doubtless by Ewan's slipping
the buckle of his belt, had dropped off at
the horse's tail, and instantly dived, passing
under the belly of the troop-horse which was
on his left hand. · But as he was obliged to
come to the surface an instant for air, the
glimpse of his tartan plaid drew the attention of the troopers, some of whom plun-

ged into the river with a total disregard to
their own safety, rushing, according to the
expression of their country, through pool and
stream, sometimes swimming their horses,
sometimes losing them and struggling for
their own lives. Others less zealous, or
more prudent, broke off in different directions, and gallopped up and down the
banks, to watch the places at which the
fugitive might possibly land. The hollow-
ing, the whooping, the calls for aid at different points, where they saw, or conceived
they saw, some vestige of him they were
seeking,—the frequent report of pistols
and carabines, fired at every object which
excited the least suspicion,—the sight of
so many horsemen riding about, in and out
of the river, and striking with their long
broadswords at whatever excited their attention, joined to the vain exertions used
by their officers to restore order and regularity ; and all this in so wild a scene, and
visible only by the imperfect twilight of

an autumn evening, made the most extraordinary hubbub I had hitherto witnessed.
I was indeed left alone to observe it, for
our whole cavalcade had dispersed in pursuit, or at least to see the event of the
search. Indeed, as I partly suspected at
the time, and afterwards learned with certainty, many of those who seemed most
active in their attempts to waylay and re-
cover the fugitive, were, in actual truth,
least desirous that he should be taken, and
only joined in the cry to increase the general confusion, and give Rob Roy a better
opportunity of escaping.

Escape, indeed, was not difficult for a
swimmer so expert as the freebooter, so
soon as he had eluded the first burst of
pursuit. At one time he was closely pressed, and several blows were made which
flashed in the water around him, the appearance much resembling one of the ot-
ter-hunts which I had seen at Osbaldistone Hall, where the animal is detected by the hounds from his being necessi-

tated to put his nose above the stream to vent or breathe, while he is enabled to elude them by getting under water again so soon as he has refreshed himself by respiration. MacGregor, however, had a trick beyond the otter; for he contrived, when very closely pursued, to disengage himself unobserved from his plaid, and suffer it to float down the stream, where in its progress it quickly attracted general attention ; many of the horsemen were thus put upon a false scent, and several shots or stabs were averted from the party for whom they were designed.

Once fairly out of view, the recovery of the prisoner became almost impossible; since, in so many places, the river was rendered inaccessible by the steepness of its banks, or the thickets of alders, poplar, and birch, which, over-hanging its banks, prevented the approach of horsemen. Errors and accidents had also happened among the pursuers, whose task the approaching night rendered every mo--

ment more hopeless. Some got themselves involved in the eddies of the stream, and required the assistance of their companions to save them from drowning. Others, hurt by shot or blows in the confused meleé, implored help or threatened vengeance, and in one or two instances such accidents led to fatal strife. The trumpets, therefore, sounded the retreat, announcing that the commanding officer, with whatsoever unwillingness, had for the present relinquished hopes of the important prize which had thus unexpectedly escaped his grasp, and the troopers began slowly, reluctantly, and brawling with each other as they returned, again to assume their ranks. I could see them darkening as they formed on the southern bank of the river, whose murmurs, long drowned by the louder cries of vengeful pursuit, were now heard hoarsely mingling with the deep, discontented, and reproachful voices of the disappointed horsemen.

Hitherto I had been as it were a mere

spectator, though far from an uninterested one, of the singular scene which had passed. But now I heard a voice suddenly exclaim, " Where is the English stranger? —It was he gave Rob Roy the knife to cut the belt."

" Cleave the pock-pudding to the chafts," cried one voice.

" Weize a brace of balls through his harn pan," said a second.

" Drive three inches of cauld airn into his breaskit," shouted a third.

And I heard several horses gallopping to and fro, with the kind purpose, doubtless, of executing these denunciations. I was immediately awakened to the sense of my situation, and to the certainty that armed men, having no restraint whatever on their irritated and inflamed passions, would probably begin by shooting or cutting me down, and afterwards investigate the justice of the action. Impressed by this belief, I leaped from my horse, and turning him loose, plunged into a bush of alder trees, where, considering the advancing obscurity of the night, I thought there was little chance of my being discovered. Had I been near enough to the Duke to have invoked his personal protection, I would have done so; but he had already commenced his retreat, and I saw no officer on the left bank of the river of authority sufficient to have afforded protection, in case of my surrendering myself. I thought there was no point of honour which could require, in such circumstances, an unnecessary exposure of my life. My first idea, when the tumult began to be appeased, and the clatter of the horses' feet was heard less frequently in the immediate vicinity of my hiding-place, was to seek out the Duke's quarters, when all should be quiet, and give myself up to him, as a liege subject who had nothing to fear from his justice, and a stranger, who had every right to expect protection and hospitality. With this purpose I crept out of my hiding-place, and looked around me.

The twilight had now melted nearly into
darkness; few or none of the troopers were
left on my side of the Forth, and of those
who were already across it, I only heard
the distant trample of the horses' feet, and
the wailing and prolonged sound of their
trumpets, which rung through the woods to
recal stragglers.   Here, therefore, I was
left in a situation of considerable difficulty.
I had no horse, and the deep and wheeling
stream of the river, rendered turbid by the
late tumult of which its channel had been
the scene, and seeming yet more so under
the doubtful influence of an imperfect
moonlight, had no inviting influence for a
pedestrian by no means accustomed to
wade rivers, and who had lately seen horsemen weltering, in this dangerous passage,
up to the very saddle laps.   At the same
time, my prospect, if I remained on the side
of the river on which I then stood, could
be no other than of concluding the various
fatigues of this day and the preceding
night, by passing-that which was now clo-

sing in *al fresco* on the side of a Highland hill.

After a moment's reflection, I began to consider that Fairservice, who had doubtless crossed the river with the other domestics, according to his forward and impertinent custom of putting himself always among the foremost, could not fail to satisfy the Duke, or the competent authorities, respecting my rank and situation; and that, therefore, my character did not require my immediate appearance, at the risk of being drowned in the river,—of being unable to trace the march of the squadron, in case of my reaching the other side in safety,—or, finally, of being cut down, right or wrong, by some straggler, who might think such a piece of good service a convenient excuse for not sooner rejoining his ranks. I therefore resolved to measure my steps back to the little inn, where I had passed the preceding night. I had nothing to apprehend from Rob Roy.

He was now at liberty, and I was certain, in case of my falling in with any of his people, the news of his escape would ensure me protection. I might thus also show, that I had no intention to desert Mr Jarvie in the delicate situation in which he had engaged himself, chiefly on my account. And lastly, it was only in this quarter that I could hope to learn tidings concerning Rashleigh and my father's papers, which had been the original cause of an expedition so fraught with perilous adventure. I therefore abandoned all thoughts of crossing the Forth that evening; and, turning my back on the Fords of Frew, began to retrace my steps toward the little village of Aberfoil.

A sharp frost wind, which made itself heard and felt from time to time, removed the clouds of mist which might otherwise have slumbered till morning on the valley; and, though it could not totally disperse the clouds of vapour, yet threw them in confused and changeful masses, now hovering round the heads of the mountains, now filling, as with a dense and voluminous stream of smoke, the various deep gullies where masses of the composite rock, or *brescia*, tumbling in fragments from the cliffs, have rushed to the valley, leaving each behind its course a rent and torn ravine resembling a deserted water-course. The moon, which was now high, and twinkled with all the vivacity of a frosty atmosphere, silvered the windings of the river and the peaks and precipices which the mist left visible, while her beams seemed as it were absorbed by the fleecy whiteness of the mist, where it lay thick and condensed; and gave to the more light and vapoury specks, which were elsewhere visible, a sort of filmy transparency resembling the lightest veil of silver gauze. Despite the uncertainty of my situation, a view so romantic, joined to the active and inspiring influence of the frosty atmosphere, elevated my spirits while it braced my nerves. I felt an

inclination to cast care away, and bid defiance to danger, and involuntarily whistled, by way of cadence to my steps, which
my feeling of the cold led me to accele-
rate, and I felt the pulse of existence beat
prouder and higher in proportion as I felt
confidence in my own strength, courage,
and resources. I was so much lost in these
thoughts, and in the feelings which they
excited, that two horsemen came up behind me without my hearing their approach, until one was on each side of me,
when the left-hand rider, pulling up his
horse, addressed me in the English tongue.
" So ho, friend, whither so late ?"

" To my supper and bed at Aberfoil," I
replied.

" Are the passes open ?" he enquired,
with the same commanding tone of voice.

" I do not know," I replied ; " I shall
learn when I get there ; but," I added, the
fate of Morris recurring to my recollection, " if you are an English stranger, I

advise you to turn back till daylight; there has been some disturbance in this neighbourhood, and I should hesitate to say it is perfectly safe for strangers."

" The soldiers had the worst ?—had they not ?" was the reply.

" They had indeed ; and an officer's party were destroyed or made prisoners."

" Are you sure of that ?" replied the horseman.

" As sure as that I hear you speak," I replied. " I was an unwilling spectator of the skirmish."

" Unwilling ? Were you not engaged in it, then ?"

" Certainly no," I replied, " I was detained by the king's officer."

" On what suspicion ? and who are you ? or what is your name ?" he continued.

" I really do not know, sir," said I, " why I should answer so many questions to an unknown stranger. I have told you enough to convince you that you are going

into a dangerous and distracted country.—
If you chuse to proceed, it is your own affair ; but as I ask you no questions respecting your name and business, you will
oblige me by making no enquiries after
mine."

"Mr Francis Osbaldistone," said the
other rider, in a voice, the tones of which
thrilled through every nerve of my body,
"should not whistle his favourite airs when
he wishes to remain undiscovered."

And Diana Vernon, for she, wrapped in
a horseman's cloak, was the last speaker,
whistled in playful mimicry the second
part of the tune, which was on my lips
when they came up.

"Good God !" I exclaimed, like one
thunderstruck, "can it be you, Miss Vernon, on such a spot—at such an hour—
in such a lawless country—in such"——

"In such a masculine dress, you would
say.—But what would you have ?—The phi-
losophy of the excellent Corporal Nym is the

best after all—things must be as they may
—*pauca verba.*"

While she was thus speaking, I eagerly
took advantage of an unusually bright
gleam of moonshine, to study the appearance of her companion, for it may be easily supposed, that finding Miss Vernon in a
place so solitary, engaged in a journey so
dangerous, and under the protection of
one gentleman only, were circumstances to
excite every feeling of jealousy, as well as
surprise. The rider did not speak with
the deep melody of Rashleigh's voice; his
tones were more high and commanding;
he was taller, moreover, as he sate on horseback, than that first-rate object of my hatred and suspicion. Neither did the stranger's address resemble that of any of my
other cousins; it had that indescribable
tone and manner by which we recognize a
man of sense and breeding, even in the first
few sentences he speaks.

The object of my anxiety seemed desirous to get rid of my investigation.

" Diana," he said, in a tone of mingled kindness and authority, " give your cousin his property, and not let us spend time here."

Miss Vernon had in the mean time taken out a small case, and leaning down from her horse towards me, she said, in a tone in which an effort at her usual quaint lightness of expression contended with a deeper and more grave tone of sentiment, " You see, my dear coz, I was born to be your better angel. Rashleigh has been compelled to yield up his spoil, and had we reached this same village of Aberfoil last night, as we purposed, I should have found some Highland sylph to have wafted to you all these representatives of commercial wealth. But there were giants and dragons in the way ; and errant-knights and damsels of modern times, bold though they be, must not, as of yore, run into useless danger—Do not you do so either, my dear coz."

" Diana," said her companion, " let me

once more warn you that the evening waxes late, and we are still distant from our home."

" I am coming, sir, I am coming - consider," she added, with a sigh, " how lately I have been subjected to controul—besides, I have not yet given my cousin the packet —and bid him farewell—for-ever—Yès, Frank," she said, " for *ever*—there is a gulph between us—a gulph of absolute perdition—where we go, you must not follow —what we do, you must not share in— farewell—be happy."

In the attitude in which she bent from her horse, which was a Highland poney, her face, not perhaps altogether unwillingly, touched mine—She pressed my hand, while the tear that trembled in her eye found its way to my cheek instead of her own. It was a moment never to be forgotten—inexpressibly bitter, yet mixed with a sensation of pleasure so deeply soothing and affecting, as at once to unlock all the flood-gates of the heart. It was *but* a moment, however, for instantly recovering

from the feeling to which she had involuntarily given way, she intimated to her companion she was ready to attend him, and
putting their horses to a brisk pace, they
were soon far distant from the place where
I stood.

Heaven knows, it was not apathy which
loaded my frame and my tongue so much,
that I could neither return Miss Vernon's
half embrace, nor even answer her farewell.
The word, though it rose to my tongue,
seemed to choke in my throat like the fatal
guilty, which the delinquent who makes it
his plea knows must be followed by the
doom of death. The surprise—the sorrow,
almost stupified me. I remained motionless with the packet in my hand, gazing
after them, as if endeavouring to count
the sparkles which flew from the horses'
hoofs. I continued to look after even
these had ceased to be visible, and to listen
for their footsteps long after the last distant trampling had died in my ears. At
length, tears rushed to my eyes, glazed as

they were by the exertion of straining after
what was no longer to be seen. I wiped
them mechanically, and almost without being aware that they were flowing, but they
came thicker and thicker—I felt the tight-
ening of the throat and breast, the *hysterica
passio* of poor Lear ; and, sitting down by
the wayside, I shed a flood of the first and
most bitter tears which had flowed from
my eyes since childhood.

CHAPTER VII.

Dangle. Egad, I think the interpreter is the harder to be understood of the two.

Critic.

I HAD scarce given vent to my feelings in this paroxysm, ere I was ashamed of my weakness. I remembered that I had been for some time endeavouring to regard Diana Vernon, when her idea intruded itself on my remembrance, as a friend, for whose welfare I should indeed always be anxious, but with whom I could have little further communication. But the almost unrepressed tenderness of her manner, joined to the romance of our sudden meeting where it was so little to have been expected, were circumstances which threw me entirely off my guard. I recovered, however, sooner than might have been expected, and

4

without giving myself time accurately to examine my motives, I resumed the path on which I had been travelling when over-taken by this strange and unexpected apparition.

· " I am not," was my reflection, " transgressing her injunction so pathetically given, since I am but pursuing my own journey by the only open route. If I have·succeeded in recovering my father's property, it still remains incumbent on me -to see my Glasgow friend delivered from the situation in which he has involved - himself on my account ; besides, what other place of rest can I obtain for the night excepting at the little inn of Aberfoil ? They also must stop there, since it is impossible for travellers on horseback to go farther— Well then we shall meet again—meet for the last time perhaps—but I shall see and hear her—I shall learn who this happy man is who exercises over her the authority of a husband—I shall learn if there remains, in the difficult course in which she seems engaged, any difficulty which my efforts may remove, or aught that I can do to express my gratitude for her generosity —for her disinterested friendship."

As I reasoned thus with myself, colouring, with every plausible pretext which occurred to my ingenuity, my passionate desire once more to see and converse with my cousin, I was suddenly hailed by a touch on the shoulder; and the deep voice of a Highlander, who, walking still faster than I, though I was proceeding at a smart pace, accosted me with, " A braw night, Maister Osbaldistone—we have met at the mirk hour before now."

There was no mistaking the tone of MacGregor; he had escaped the pursuit of his enemies, and was in full retreat to his own wilds and to his adherents. He had also contrived to arm himself, probably at the house of some secret adherent, for he had a musket on his shoulder, and the usual Highland weapons by his side. To have found myself alone with such a

11

character in such a situation, and at this late hour in the evening, might not have been pleasant to me in any ordinary mood of mind ; for, though habituated to think of Rob Roy in rather a friendly point of view, I will confess frankly that I never heard him speak but what it seemed to thrill my blood. The intonation of the mountaineers gives a habitual depth and hollowness to the sound of their words, owing to the guttural expression so common in their native language, and they usually speak with a good deal of emphasis. To these national peculiarities Rob Roy added a sort of hard indifference of accent and manner, expressive of a mind neither to be daunted, nor surprised, nor affected by what passed before him, however dreadful, however sudden, however afflicting. Habitual danger, with unbounded confidence in his own strength and sagacity, had rendered him indifferent to fear ; and the unlawful and precarious life which he led had blunted, though its dangers and errors had not destroyed, his feelings for others. And it was to be remembered, that I had very lately seen the followers of this man commit a cruel slaughter on an unarmed and suppliant individual.

Yet such was the state of my mind, that I welcomed the company of the outlaw-leader as a relief to my own overstrained and painful thoughts ; and was not without hopes, that through his means I might obtain some clew of guidance through the maze in which my fate had involved me. I therefore answered his greeting cordially, and congratulated him on his late escape in circumstances when escape seemed impossible.

" Ay," he replied, " there is as much between the craig and the woodie as there is between the cup and the lip. But my peril was less than you may think, being a stranger to this country. Of those that were summoned to take me, and to keep me, and to retake me again, there was a moiety, as Cousin Nicol Jarvie calls it, that had nae will that I suld be either taen, or keepit fast, or retaen ; and of the t'other moiety, there was ae half was feared to-stir me; and so I had only like the fourth part of fifty or sixty men to deal withal."

" And enough too, I should think," replied I.

" I dinna ken that," said he ; " but I 'ken, that turn every ill-willer that I had amang them out upon the green before the Clachan of Aberfoil, I wad find them play with broad-sword and target, one down and another come on."

He now enquired into my adventures since we entered his country, and laughed heartily at my account of the battle we had in the inn, and at the exploits of the Baillie with the red-hot poker.

. " Let Glasgow Flourish !" he exclaimed. " The curse of Cromwell on me, if I wad hae wished better sport than to see cousin Nicol Jarvie singe Iverach's plaid; like a sheep's head between a pair of tongs. But my cousin Jarvie," he added more gravely, " has some gentleman's bluid in his veins, although he has been unhappily bred up to a peaceful and mechanical craft, which could not but blunt any pretty man's spirit. —Ye may estimate the reason why I could not receive you at the Clachan of Aberfoil, as I purposed.—They had made a fine hose-net for me when I was absent twa or three days at Glasgow, upon the king's business —but I think I broke up the league about their lugs—they'll no be able to hound one clan against another as they hae dune. —I hope sune to see the day when a' Hie-landmen will stand shouther to shouther.— But what chanced next?"

I gave him an account of the arrival of Captain Thornton and his party, and the ar-rest of the Baillie and myself, under pretext of our being suspicious persons; and upon his more special enquiry, I recollected the officer had mentioned that, besides my name sounding suspicious in his ears, he had orders to secure an old and young person, resembling our description. This again moved the outlaw's risibility.

" As man lives by bread," he said, " the buzzards have mista'en my friend the Bàillie for his Excellency, and you for Diana Vernon — O the most egregious night-owls !"

" Miss Vernon ?" said I, with hesitation, and trembling for the answer—" Does she still bear that name ?—She passed but now, along with a gentleman who seemed to use a style of authority."

" Ay, ay !" answered Rob, " she's under lawfu' authority now, and full time, for she was a daft hempie—But she's a mettle quean.—It's a pity his Excellency is a thought eldern. The like o' yoursell, or my son Rob, or Hamish, wad be mair sortable in point of years."

Here then was a complete downfall of those castles of cards which my fancy had, in despite of my reason, so often amused herself with building. Although in truth I had scarce any thing else to expect, since

I could not suppose that Diana could be travelling in such a country, at such an hour, with any but one who had a legal title to protect her, I did not feel the blow less severely when it came, and MacGregor's voice, urging me to pursue my story, sounded in my ears without conveying any exact import to my mind.

" You are ill," he said, at length, after he had spoken twice without receiving an answer ; " this day's wark has been ower muckle for ane doubtless unused to sic things."

The tone of kindness in which this was spoken recalling me to myself, and to the necessities of my situation, I continued my narrative as well as I could.—Rob Roy expressed great exultation at the successful skirmish in the pass.

" They say," he observed, " that king's chaff is better than other folks corn ; but I think that canna be said o' king's soldiers, if they let themselves be beaten wi' a wheen auld carles that are past fighting, and bairns

that are no come till't, and wives wi' their
rocks and distaffs, the very wally-dragles
o' the countryside—and Dougal Gregor,
too, wha wad hae thought there had been
as muckle sense in his tatty pow, that near
had a better covering than his ain shaggy
hassock of hair—But say away—though I
dread what's to come neist, for my Helen's
an incarnate devil when her bluid's up—
puir thing, she has ower muckle reason."

I observed as much delicacy as I could
in communicating to him the usage we
had received, but I obviously saw the detail gave him great pain.

. " I wad rather than a thousand merks,"
he said, " that I had been at hame—to
misguide strangers, and forbye a', my ain
natural cousin that had shewed me sic kindness—I wad rather they had burned half
the Lennox in their folly—but this comes
o' trusting women and their bairns, that
have neither measure nor reason in their
dealings—however, it's a' owing to that dog
of a gauger, wha betrayed me by pretend-

ing a message from your cousin Rashleigh,
to meet him on the king's affairs, whilk I
thought was very like to be anent Garschat.
tachin and a party of the Lennox declaring
themselves for King James. Faith, but I
kenn'd I was clean beguiled when I heard
the Duke was there; and when they strapped
the horse-girth ower my arms, I might hae
judged what was biding me, for I kenned
your kinsman, being, wi' pardon, a slippry
loon himsell, is prone to employ those of his
ain kidney—I wish he mayna hae been at the
bottom o' the ploy himsell—I thought the
chield Morris looked devilish queer when
I determined he should remain a wad, or
hostage, for my safe back-coming—but I
am come back, nae thanks to him or them
that employed him, and the question is,
how the collector-loon is to win back himsell—I promise him it will not be without
ransom."

"Morris," said I, "has already paid the
last ransom which mortal man can owe."

"Eh! What?" exclaimed my companion

hastily, " I trust it was in the skirmish he
was killed."

" He was slain in cold blood, after the
fight was over, Mr Campbell."

" Cold blood ?—Damnation !" he said,
muttering betwixt his teeth—" How fell
that, sir ?—Speak out, sir, and do not Master or Campbell me—my foot is on my native heath, and my name is MacGregor."

His passions were obviously irritated ;
but, without noticing the rudeness of his
tone, I gave him a short and distinct account of the death of Morris. He struck
the butt of his gun with great vehemence
against the ground, and broke out, " I vow
to God ! such a deed might make one for-
swear kin, clan, country, wife, and bairns !
And yet the villain wrought long for it.
And what is the difference between warst-
ling below the water wi' a stane about your
neck, and wavering in the wind wi' a tether
round it ?—it's but choking after a', and he
drees the doom he ettled for me. I could
hae wished, though, they had rather putten

a ball through him, or a dirk; for the fashion
of removing him will give rise to mony idle
clavers—But every wight has his weird, and
we maun a' dee when our day comes—And
naebody will deny that Helen MacGregor
has deep wrongs to avenge."

So saying, he seemed to dismiss the
theme altogether from his mind, and proceeded to enquire how I got free from the
party in whose hands he had seen me.

My story was soon told; and I added
the episode of my having recovered the
papers of my father, though I dared not
trust my voice to name the name of
Diana.

" I was sure ye wad get them," said
MacGregor; " the letter ye brought me
contained his Excellency's pleasure to that
effect; and nae doubt it was my will to
have aided in it.   And I asked ye up into
this glen on the very errand.   But it's like
his Excellency has forgathered wi' Rashleigh sooner than I expected."

The first part of this answer was what most forcibly struck me.

"Was the letter I brought you, then, from this person you call his Excellency? Who is he? and what is his rank and proper name?"

"I am thinking," said MacGregor, "that since ye dinna ken them already, they canna be o' muckle consequence to you, and sae I shall say naething on that score. But weel I wot the letter was frae his ain hand, or, having a sort of business of my ain on my hands, being, as you weel may see, just as much as I can fairly manage, I canna say I would hae fashed mysell sae muckle about the matter."

I now recollected the lights seen in the library—the various circumstances which had excited my jealousy—the glove—the agitation of the tapestry which covered the secret passage from Rashleigh's apartment; and above all, I recollected that Diana retired, in order to write, as I then thought,

the billet to which I was to have recourse
in case of the last necessity. Her hours,
then, were not spent in solitude, but in
listening to the addresses of some desperate agent of jacobitical treason, who was
a secret resident within the mansion of
her uncle. Other young women have sold
themselves for gold, or suffered themselves
to be seduced from their first love from va-
nity; but Diana had sacrificed my affections and her own to partake the fortunes
of some desperate adventurer—to seek the
haunts of freebooters through midnight deserts, with no better hopes of rank or fortune than that mimicry of both which the
mock court of the Stuarts at St Germains
had in their power to bestow.

" I will see her," I said, " if it be possible, once more. I will argue with her as a
friend—as a kinsman—on the risk she is incurring, and I will facilitate her retreat to
France, where she may with more comfort
and propriety, as well as safety, abide the
issue of the turmoils which the political tre-

panner, to whom she has united her fate, is doubtless busied in putting into motion.

" I conclude then," I said to MacGregor, after about five minutes silence on both sides, " that his Excellency, since you give me no other name for him, was residing in Osbaldistone Hall at the same time with myself?"

" To be sure—to be sure—and in the young lady's apartment, as best reason was." This gratuitous information was adding gall to bitterness. " But few," added MacGregor, " kenn'd he was derned there save Rashleigh and Sir Hildebrand; for you were out o' the question; and the young lads haena wit aneugh to ca' the cat frae the cream—But it's a bra' auld-fashioned house; and what I specially admire, is the abundance o' holes and bores and concealments—ye could put twenty or thirty men in ae corner, and a family might live a week without finding them out—whilk, nae doubt, may on occasion be a special convenience. I wish we had the like o'

Osbaldistone-Hall on the braes o' Craig
Roystone—But we maun gar woods and
caves serve the like o' us puir Hieland
bodies."

" I suppose his Excellency," said I,
" was privy to the first accident which
befel"——

I could not help hesitating a moment.

" Ye were going to say Morris," said
Rob Roy coolly, for he was too much accustomed to deeds of violence for the agitation he had first expressed to be of long
continuance. " I used to laugh heartily at
that reik, but I'll hardly hae the heart to
do't again, since the ill-farr'd accident at
the Loch—Na, na, his Excellency kenn'd
nought o' that ploy—it was a' managed
atween Rashleigh and mysel. But the sport
that came after—and Rashleigh's shift o'
turning the suspicion aff himsel upon you,
that he had nae grit favour to frae the beginning—and then Miss Die, she maun hae
us sweep up a' our spiders webs again, and
set you out o' the justice's claws—and then

the frightened craven, Morris, that was
scared out o' his seven senses by seeing
the real man when he was charging the
untrue—and the gowk of a clerk—and the
drunken carle of a justice—Ohon! ohon!
—mony a laugh that job's gi'en me—and
now, a' that I can do for the puir devil is
to get some messes said for his soul."

"May I ask," said I, "how Miss Vernon came to have so much influence over
Rashleigh and his accomplices as to de-
range your projected plan?"

"Mine? it was none of mine. No man
can say I ever laid my burden on other
folks shoulders—it was a' Rashleigh's doings—But, undoubtedly, she had great influence wi' us baith on account of his Excellency's affection, as weel as that she
kenn'd far ower mony secrets to be light-
lied in a matter o' that kind.—Deil tak
him," he ejaculated, by way of summing
up, "that gi'es women either secret to keep
or power to abuse—fules shouldna hae
chapping sticks."

We were now within a quarter of a mile from the village, when three Highlanders, springing upon us with presented arms, commanded us to stand and tell our business. The single word *Gregaragh*, in the deep and commanding voice of my companion, was answered by a shout, or rather yell, of joyful recognition. One, throwing down his firelock, clasped his leader so fast round the knees, that he was unable to extricate himself, muttering, at the same time, a torrent of Gaelic gratulation, which every now and then rose into a sort of scream of gladness. The two others, after the first howling was over, set off literally with the speed of deers, contending which should first carry to the village, which a strong party of the MacGregors now occupied, the joyful news of Rob Roy's escape and return. The intelligence excited such shouts of jubilation that the very hills rung again, and young and old, men, women, and children, without dis-

tinction of sex or age, came running down
the vale to meet us, with all the tumultu-
ous speed and clamour of a mountain torrent. When I heard the rushing noise and
yells of this joyful multitude approach us,
I thought it a fitting precaution to remind
MacGregor that I was a stranger, and under his protection. He accordingly held
me fast by the hand, while the assemblage
crowded around him with such shouts of de-
voted attachment and joy at his return, as
were really affecting ; nor did he extend to
his followers what all eagerly sought, the
grasp, namely, of his hand, until he had
made them understand that I was to be
kindly and carefully used.

The mandate of the Sultan of Delhi
could not have been more promptly obeyed. Indeed, I now sustained nearly as
much inconvenience from their well-meant
attentions as formerly from their rudeness.
They would hardly allow the friend of their
leader to walk upon his own legs, so earnest

were they in affording me support and assistance upon the way, and, at length, taking advantage of a slight stumble which I
made over a stone, which the press did not
permit me to avoid, they fairly seized upon
me, and bore me in their arms in triumph
towards Mrs MacAlpine's.

On arrival before her hospitable wig-
wam, I found power and popularity had
its inconveniences in the Highlands, as
everywhere else; for, before MacGregor
could be permitted to enter the house
where he was to obtain rest and refreshment, he was obliged to relate the story
of his escape at least a dozen times over, as
I was told by an officious old man, who
chose to translate it at least as often for
my edification, and to whom I was in po-
licy obliged to seem to pay a decent degree
of attention. The audience being at length
satisfied, group after group departed to
take their bed upon the heath, or in the
neighbouring huts, some cursing the Duke

and Garschattachin, some lamenting the misfortune of Ewan of Brigglands, incurred by his friendship to MacGregor, but all agreeing that the escape of Rob Roy himself lost nothing in comparison with the exploit of any one of their chiefs since the days of Dougal-Ciar, the founder of his line.

The friendly outlaw, now taking me by the arm, conducted me into the interior of the hut. My eyes roved round its smoky recesses in quest of Diana and her companion; but they were no where to be seen, and I felt as if to make enquiries might betray some secret motives, which were best concealed. The only known countenance upon which my eyes rested, was that of the Baillie, who, seated on a stool by the fire-side, received, with a sort of reserved dignity, the welcomes of Rob Roy, the apologies which he made for his indifferent accommodation, and his enquiries after his health.

" I am pretty weel, kinsman," said the

Baillie, " indifferent weel, I thank ye ; and for accommodations, ane canna expect to carry about the Saut-Market at his tail, as a snail does his caup—and I am blythe that ye hae gotten out o' the hands o' your un-freends."

"Weel, weel then," answered Roy, "what is't ails ye, man ?—a's weel that ends weel ! —the warld will last our day—come, take a cup o' brandy—your father the deacon could tak ane at an orra time."

" It might be he might do sae, Robin, after fatigue—whilk has been my lot mair ways than ane this day. But," he continued, slowly filling up a little wooden stoup which might hold about three glasses, " he was a moderate man of his bicker, as I am mysel—Here's wussing health to ye, Robin, and your weelfare here and hereafter, and also to my cousin Helen, and to your twa hopefu' lads, of whom mair anon."

So saying, he drank up the contents of the cup with great gravity and deliberation, while MacGregor winked aside to me, as if in ridicule of the air of wisdom and supe-

rior authority which the Baillie assumed towards him in their intercourse, and which
he exercised when Rob was at the head of
his armed clan, in full as great, or a greater
degree, than when he was at the Baillie's
mercy in the Tolbooth of Glasgow. It
seemed to me, that MacGregor wished
me, as a stranger, to understand, that if he
submitted to the tone which his kinsman
assumed, it was partly out of deference to
the rights of hospitality, but still more for
the jest's sake.

As the Baillie set down his cup he recognized me, and giving me a cordial welcome
on my return, he waived farther communication with me for the present.

" I will speak to your matters anon ; I
maun begin, as in reason, wi' those of my
kinsman.—I presume, Robin, there's naebody here will carry ought o' what I am
gaun to say to the town council or elsewhere, to my prejudice or to yours ?"

" Make yourself easy on that head, cousin Nicol," answered MacGregor ; " the

ae half o' them winna ken what ye say, and
the tother winna care—besides, that I wad
stow the tongue out o' the head o' ony o'
them that suld presume to say ower again
ony speech held wi' me in their presence."

" Aweel, cousin, sic being the case, and
Mr Osbaldistone here being a prudent
youth, and a safe friend—I'se plainly tell
ye, ye are breeding up your family to gang
an ill gate."—Then clearing his voice with
a preliminary hem, he addressed his kinsman, checking, as Malvolio proposed to do
when seated in his state, his familiar smile
with an austere regard of controul.—" Ye
ken yoursel ye haud light by the law—and
for my cousin Helen, forbye that her reception o' me this blessed day, whilk I excuse on account of perturbation of mind,
was muckle on the north side o' *friendly*,
I say (out-putting this personal reason of
complaint,) I hae that to say o' your
wife"——

" Say *nothing* of her, kinsman," said
Rob, in a grave and stern tone, " but what

is befitting a friend to say, and her husband to hear. Of me you are welcome to
say your full pleasure."

" Aweel, aweel," said the Baillie, somewhat disconcerted, " we'se let that be a
pass-over—I dinna approve of making mischief in families—But here are your twa
sons, Robin, and Hamish, whilk signifies, as
I am gi'en to understand, James—I trust
ye will call him sae in future—there comes
nae gude o' Hamishes, and Eachines, and
Angusses, except that they're the names
ane aye chances to see in the indictments
at the western circuits for cow-lifting, at
the instance of his majesty's advocate for
his majesty's interest—aweel, but the twa
lads, as I was saying, they haena sae
muckle as the ordinar grunds, man, of li-
beral education—they dinna ken the very
multiplication-table itself, whilk is the root
of a' usefu' knowledge, and they did naething but laugh and fleer at me when I
tauld them my mind on their ignorance—
It's my belief they can neither read, write,

nor cypher, if sic a thing could be believed o' ane's ain connections in a Christian land."

" " If they could, kinsman," said Mac-Gregor, with great indifference, " their learning must have come o' free will, for whar the deil was I to get them a teacher ?—wad ye hae had me put on the gate o' your Divinity-Hall at Glasgow-College, ' Wanted, a tutor for Rob Roy's bairns ?' "

" Na, kinsman," replied Mr Jarvie, " but ye might hae sent the lads whar they could hae learned the fear o' God, and the usages of civilized creatures. They are as ignorant as the kyloes ye used to drive to market, or the very English churles that ye sauld them to, and can do naething whatever to purpose."

" Umph !" answered Rob ; " Hamish can bring doun a black cock when he's on the wing wi' a single bullet, and Rob can drive a dirk through a twa-inch board."

" Sae muckle the waur for them, cousin ! Sae muckle the waur for them baith !" answered the Glasgow merchant in a tone of

great decision; "an they ken naething better than that, they had better no ken that
neither. Tell me yoursell, Rob, what has
a' this cutting, and stabbing, and shooting
dune for ye? and were na ye a happier
man at the tail o' your nowte-bestial, when
ye were in an honest calling, than ever ye
hae been since, at the head o' your Hieland
kernes and gally-glasses?"

I observed that MacGregor, while his
well-meaning kinsman spoke to him in this
manner, turned and writhed his body like
a man who indeed suffers pain, but is determined no groan shall escape his lips;
and I longed for an opportunity to inter-
rupt the well-meant, but, as it was obvious
to me, quite mistaken strain, in which Jarvie addressed this extraordinary person.
The dialogue, however, came to an end
without my interference.

" And sae," said the Baillie, " I hae
been thinking, Rob, that as it may be ye
are ower deep in the black book to win a
pardon, and ower auld to mend yoursell,

that it wad be a pity to bring up twa hopefu' lads to sic a godless trade as your ain,
and I wad blythely tak them for prentices
at the loom, as I began mysell and my father the deacon afore me, though, praise
to the Giver, I only trade now as whole-
sale dealer—And—and"——

He saw a storm gathering on Rob's brow,
which probably induced him to throw in,
as a sweetener of an obnoxious proposition,
what he had reserved to crown his own generosity, had it been embraced as an acceptable one. "And Robin, lad, ye needna
look sae glum, for I'll pay the prentice-
fee, and never plague ye for the thousand
merks neither."

"*Ceade millia diaoul*, hundred thousand
devils!" exclaimed Rob, rising and stri-
ding through the hut. "My sons weavers!
—*Millia molligheart!* but I would see every
loom in Glasgow, beam, traddles, and shut-
tles, burned in hell fire sooner!"

With some difficulty I made the Baillie,

who was preparing a reply, comprehend the risk and impropriety of pressing our host on this topic, and in a minute he recovered, or reassumed, his serenity of temper.

" But you mean weel—you mean weel," said he ; " so gie me your hand, Nicol, and if ever I put my sons apprentice, I will gie you the refusal o' them. And, as you say, there's the thousand merks to be sattled between us. Here, Eachin MacAnaleister, bring me my sporran."

The person he addressed, a tall, strong mountaineer, who seemed to act as Mac-Gregor's lieutenant, brought from some place of safety a large leathern pouch, such as Highlanders of rank wear before them when in full dress, made of the skin of the sea otter, richly garnished with silver ornaments and studs.

" I advise no man to attempt opening this sporran till he has my secret," said Rob Roy, and then twisting one button in one direction, and another in another, pulling one stud upward, and pressing another downward, the mouth of the purse, which was bound with massive silver-plate, opened and gave admittance to his hand. He made me remark, as if to break short the subject on which Baillie Jarvie had spoken, that a small steel pistol was concealed within the purse, the trigger of which was connected with the mounting, and made part of the machinery, so that the weapon would certainly be discharged, and in all probability its contents lodged in the person of any one, who, being unacquainted with the secret, should tamper with the lock which secured his treasure. " This," said he, touching the pistol—" this is the keeper of my privy purse."

The simplicity of the contrivance to secure a furred pouch, which could have been ripped open without any attempt on the spring, reminded me of the verses in the Odyssey, where Ulysses, in a yet ruder age, is content to secure his property by casting a curious and involved complication of cordage around the sea-chest in which it was deposited.

The Baillie put on his spectacles to examine the mechanism, and when he had done, returned it with a smile, and a sigh, observing, "Ah! Rob, had ither folk's purses been as weel guarded, I doubt if your sporran wad hae been as weel filled as it kythes to be by the weight."

" Never mind, kinsman," said Rob, laughing, " it will aye open for a friend's necessity, or to pay a just due—and here," he added, pulling out a rouleau of gold, " here is your ten hundred merks—count them, and see that you are full and justly paid."

Mr Jarvie took the money in silence, and weighing it in his hand for an instant, laid it on the table, and replied, " Rob, I canna tak it—I downa intromit with it—there can nae gude come o't—I hae seen ower weel the day what sort of a gate your gowd is made in—ill got gear ne'er prospered;

and to be plain wi' you, I winna meddle wi't—it looks as there might be bluid on't."

" Troutsho," said the outlaw, affecting an indifference which, perhaps, he did not altogether feel, " it's gude French gowd, and ne'er was in Scotchman's pouch before mine—look at them, man—they are a' louis d'ors, bright and bonnie as the day they were coined."

" The waur, the waur—just sae muckle the waur, Robin," replied the Baillie, averting his eyes from the money, though, like Cæsar on the Lupercal, his fingers seemed to itch for it—" Rebellion is waur than witchcraft, or robbery either; there's gospel warrant for't."

" Never mind the warrant, kinsman," said the freebooter; " you come by the gowd honestly, and in payment of a just debt— if came from the one king, you may gie it to the other, if ye like, and it will just serve for a weakening of the enemy, and in the point where puir King James is weak-

est too, for, God knows, he has hands and
hearts aneugh, but I doubt he wants the
siller."

" He'll no get mony Hielanders then,
Robin," said Mr Jarvie, as, again replacing
his spectacles on his nose, he undid the
rouleau, and began to count its contents.

" Nor Lowlanders neither," said Mac-
Gregor, arching his eyebrow; and, as he
looked at me, directing a glance towards
Mr Jarvie, who, all unconscious of the ridicule, weighed each piece with habitual
scrupulosity; and having told twice over
the sum, which amounted to the discharge
of his debt, principal and interest, he returned three pieces to buy his kinswoman a
gown, as he expressed himself, and a brace
more for the two bairns, as he called them,
requesting they might buy any thing they
liked with them except gunpowder. The
Highlander stared at his kinsman's unexpected generosity, but courteously accept-
ted his gift, which he deposited for the
time in his well-secured pouch.

9

The Baillie next produced the original
bond for the debt, on the back of which he
had written a formal discharge, which, having subscribed himself, he requested me
to sign as a witness. I did so, and Baillie
Jarvie was looking anxiously around for
another, the Scottish law requiring the
subscription of two witnesses to validate
either a bond or acquittance. " You will
hardly find a man that can write save ourselves within these three miles," said Rob,
" but I'll settle the matter as easily ;" and,
taking the paper from before his kinsman,
he threw it in the fire. Baillie Jarvie
stared in his turn, but his kinsman continued, " That's a Hieland settlement of accounts—the time might come, cousin, were
I to keep a' these charges and discharges,
that friends might be brought into trouble
for having dealt with me."

The Baillie attempted no reply to this
argument, and our supper now appeared in
a style of abundance, and even delicacy,
which, for the place, might be considered

as extraordinary. The greater part of the provisions were cold, intimating they had been prepared at some distance ; and there were some bottles of good French wine to relish pasties of various sorts of game, as well as other dishes. I remarked that Mac-Gregor, while doing the honours of the table with great and anxious hospitality, prayed us to excuse the circumstance that some particular dish or pasty had been infringed on before it was presented to us. " Ye must know," said he to Mr Jarvie, but without looking towards me, " you are not the only guests this night in the Mac-Gregor's country, whilk, doubtless, ye will believe, since my wife and the twa lads would otherwise have been maist ready to attend you, as weel beseems them."

Baillie Jarvie looked as if he felt glad at any circumstance which occasioned their absence, and I should have been entirely of his opinion, had it not been that the outlaw's apology seemed to imply they were in attendance on Diana and her com-

panion, whom even in my thoughts I could
not bear to designate as her husband.

While the unpleasant ideas arising from
this suggestion counteracted the good ef-
fects of appetite, welcome, and good cheer,
I remarked that Rob Roy's attention had
extended itself to providing us better bedding than we had enjoyed the night before. Two of the least fragile of the bed-
steads, which stood by the wall of the hut,
had been stuffed with heath, then in full
flower, so artificially arranged, that the
flowers being uppermost, afforded a ma-
tress at once elastic and fragrant. Cloaks,
and such bedding as could be collected,
stretched over this vegetable couch, made
it both soft and warm. The Baillie seemed
exhausted by fatigue. I resolved to adjourn my communication to him until next
morning; and therefore suffered him to betake himself to bed so soon as he had finish-
ed a plentiful supper. Though tired and
harrassed, I did not myself feel the same
disposition to sleep, but rather a restless

and feverish anxiety, which led to some farther discourse betwixt me and Mac-Gregor.

CHAPTER VIII.

A hopeless darkness settles o'er my fate:
I've seen the last look of her heavenly eyes,—
I've heard the last sound of her blessed voice,—
I've seen her fair form from my sighs depart:
My doom is closed.

BASIL.

" I KEN not what to make of you, Mr Osbaldistone," said MacGregor, as he pushed the flask towards me. " You eat not, you show no wish for rest; and yet you drink not, though that flask of Bourdeaux might have come out of Sir Hildebrand's ain cellar. Had you been always as abstinent, you would have escaped the deadly hatred of your cousin Rashleigh."

" Had I been always prudent," said I, blushing at the scene he recalled to my recollection, " I should have escaped a worse evil—the reproach of my own conscience."

MacGregor cast a keen and somewhat fierce glance on me, as if to read whether the reproof which he evidently felt had been intentionally conveyed. He saw that I was thinking of myself, not of him, and turned his face toward the fire with a deep sigh. I followed his example, and each remained for a few minutes wrapt in his own painful reverie. All in the hut were now asleep, or at least silent, excepting ourselves.

MacGregor first broke silence, in the tone of one who takes up his determination to enter on a painful subject. " My cousin Nicol Jarvie means well," he said, " but he presses ower hard on the temper and situation of a man like me, considering what I have been—what I have been forced to become—and above all, that which has forced me to become what I am."

" He paused; and, though feeling the delicate nature of the discussion in which the conversation was like to engage me, I could not help replying, that I did not doubt his present situation had much which must be most unpleasant to his feelings. "I should be happy to learn," I added, " that there is an honourable chance of your escaping from it."

" You speak like a boy," returned Mac-Gregor, in a low tone that growled like distant thunder—" like a boy, who thinks the auld gnarled oak can be twisted as easily as the young sapling. Can I forget that I have been branded as an outlaw,— stigmatized as a traitor,—a price set on my head as if I had been a wolf,—my family treated as the dam and cubs of the hill-fox, whom all may torment, vilify, degrade, and insult;—the very name which came to me from a long and noble line of martial ancestors, denounced, as if it were a spell to conjure up the devil with ?"

As he went on in this manner, I could plainly see, that, by the enumeration of his wrongs, he was lashing himself up into a rage, in order to justify in his own eyes the errors they had led him into. In this he perfectly succeeded ; his light grey eyes, contracting alternately and dilating their pupils, until they seemed actually to flash with flame, while he thrust forward and drew back his foot, grasped the hilt of his dirk, extended his arm, clenched his fist, and finally rose from his seat.

" And they *shall* find," he said, in the same muttered, but deep tone of stifled passion, " that the name they have dared to proscribe—that the name of MacGregor *is* a spell to raise the wild devil withal.— *They* shall hear of my vengeance, that would scorn to listen to the story of my wrongs— The miserable Highland drover, bankrupt, barefooted,—stripped of all, dishonoured and hunted down, because the avarice of others grasped at more than that poor all could pay, shall burst on them in an awful

change. : They that scoffed at the grovel-
ling worm, and trode upon him, may cry
and howl when they see the stoop of the
flying and fiery-mouthed'dragon.—But why
do I speak of all this?" he said, sitting
down again, and in a calmer tone—" Only
ye may opine it frets my patience, Mr Osbaldistone, to be hunted like an otter, or a
sealgh, or a salmon upon the shallows, and
that by my very friends and neighbours;
and to have as many sword-cuts made, and
pistols flashed at me, as I had this day in
the ford of Avondow, would try a saint's
temper, much more a Highlander's, who
are not famous for that gude gift, as ye
may hae heard, Mr Osbaldistone.—But ae
thing bides wi' me o' what Nicol said—I'm
vexed for the bairns—I'm vexed when I
think o' Robert and Hamish living their
father's life." And yielding to despondence
on account of his sons, which he felt not
upon his own, the father rested his head
on his hand.

I was much affected, Will.—All my life

long I have been more melted by the distress under which a strong, proud, and
powerful mind is compelled to give way,
than by the more easily excited sorrows of
softer dispositions. The desire of aiding
him rushed strongly on my mind, notwithstanding the apparent difficulty, and even
impossibility of the task.

"We have extensive connections abroad,"
said I; "might not your sons, with some
assistance—and they are well entitled to
what my father's house can give—find an
honourable resource in foreign service?"

I believe my countenance shewed signs
of sincere emotion; but my companion, taking me by the hand, as I was going to speak
farther, said, "I thank—I thank ye—but let
us say nae mair o' this. I did not think the
eye of man would again have seen a tear on
MacGregor's eye-lash." He dashed the mois-
ture from his long grey eye-lash and shaggy
red eye-brow with the back of his hand.
"To-morrow morning," he said, "we'll
talk of this, and we will talk, too, of your

affairs—for we are early starters in the dawn, even when we have the luck to have gude beds to sleep in. Will ye not pledge me in a grace cup ?" I declined the invitation.

" Then, by the soul of St Maronoch ! I must pledge myself," and he poured out and swallowed at least half a quart of wine.

I laid myself down to repose, resolving to delay my own enquiries until his mind should be in a more composed state. Indeed, so much had this singular man possessed himself of my imagination, that I felt it impossible to avoid watching him for some minutes after I had flung myself on my heath mattress to seeming rest. He walked up and down the hut, crossed himself from time to time, muttering over some Latin prayer of the catholic church ; then wrapped himself in his plaid, with his naked sword on one side, and his pistol on the other, so disposing the folds of his mantle, that he could start up in a moment's warning, with a weapon in either hand, ready for instant combat. In a few minutes his

heavy breathing announced that he was
fast asleep. Overpowered by fatigue, and
stunned by the various unexpected and
extraordinary scenes of the day, I, in my
turn, was soon overpowered by a slumber
deep and overwhelming, from which, notwithstanding every cause for watchfulness,
I did not awake till the next morning.

When I opened my eyes, and recollected
my situation, I found that MacGregor had
already left the hut. I awakened the Baillie, who, after many a snort and groan, and
some heavy complaints of the soreness of his
bones, in consequence of the unwonted exertions of the preceding day, was at length
able to comprehend the joyful intelligence,
that the assets carried off by Rashleigh Osbaldistone had been safely recovered. The
instant he understood my meaning he forgot all his grievances, and bustling up in a
great hurry, proceeded to compare the contents of the packet, which I put into his
hands, with Mr Owen's memorandum, muttering as he went, " Right, right—the real

K 2

thing—Baillie and Whittington—where's Baillie and Whittington—seven hundred, six, and eight—exact to a fraction—Pollock and Peelman—twenty-eight—seven— exact—Praise be blest!—Grub and Grinder—better men cannot be—three hundred and seventy—Gliblad—twenty, I doubt Gliblad's ganging—Slipprytongue—Slipprytongue's gaen—but they are sma sums —sma sums—the rests a' right—Praise be blest! we have got the stuff, and may leave this doleful country. I shall never think on Loch-Hard but the thought will gar me grew again."

"I am sorry, cousin," said MacGregor, who entered the hut during the last observation, "I have not been altogether in the circumstances to make your reception sic as I could have desired—natheless, if you would condescend to visit my puir dwelling"——

"Muckle obliged, muckle obliged," answered Mr Jarvie, very hastily. "But we maun be ganging—we maun be jogging,

Mr Osbaldistone and me—business canna wait."

" Aweel, kinsman," replied the High-lander, " ye ken our fashion—foster the guest that comes—further him that maun gang.—But ye cannot return by Drymen— I must set ye on the Loch, and boat ye ower to the Ferry o' Balloch, and send your nags round to meet ye there—It's a maxim of a wise man never to return by the same road he came, providing another's free to him."

" Ay, ay, Rob, that's ane o' the maxims ye learned when ye were a drover—ye caredna to face the tenants where your beasts had been taking a rug of their moor-land grass in the bye ganging—and I doubt your road's waur marked now than it was then."

" The mair need not to travel it ower often, kinsman," replied Rob; " but I'se send round your nags to the ferry wi' Dougal, wha is converted for that pur-pose into the Baillie's man, coming—not

from Aberfoil or Rob Roy's country, but
on a quiet jaunt from Stirling.—See, here
he is."

"I wadna hae kenn'd the creature," said
Mr Jarvie ; nor indeed was it easy to recognize the wild Highlander when he appeared before the door of the cottage, at-
tired in a hat, periwig, and riding-coat,
which had once called Andrew Fairservice
master, and mounted on the Baillie's horse,
and leading mine. He received his last orders from his master to avoid certain places,
where he might be exposed to suspicion—
to collect what intelligence he could in the
course of his journey, and to await our coming at an appointed place, near the ferry
of Balloch.

At the same time, MacGregor invited us
to accompany him upon our own road, assuring us that we must necessarily march a
few miles before breakfast, and recommending a dram of brandy as a proper introduction to the journey, in which he was pled-

ged by the Baillie, who pronounced it " an unlawful and perilous habit to begin the day wi' spirituous liquors, except to defend the stomach (whilk was a tender part,) against the morning mist ; in whilk case his father the deacon had recommended a dram, by precept and example."

" Very true, kinsman," replied Rob, " for which reason we, who are Children of the Mist, have a right to drink brandy from morning till night."

The Baillie, thus refreshed, was mounted on a small Highland poney ; another was offered for my use, which, however, I declined, and we resumed, under very different guidance and auspices, our journey of the preceding day.

Our escort consisted of MacGregor, and five or six of the handsomest, best armed, and most athletic mountaineers of his band, and whom he had generally in immediate attendance upon his own person.

When we approached the pass, the scene

of the skirmish of the preceding day, and
of the still more direful deed which followed it, MacGregor hastened to speak, as it
were, rather to what he knew must be necessarily passing in my mind, than to any
thing I had said—he spoke, in short, to my
thoughts, and not to my words.

" You must think hardly of us, Mr Osbaldistone, and it is not natural that it
should be otherwise.—But remember, at
least, we have not been unprovoked—we
are a rude and an ignorant, and it may be
a violent and passionate, but we are not a
cruel people—the land might be at peace
and in law for us, did they allow us to enjoy the blessings of peaceful law.—But we
have been a persecuted people."

" And persecution," said the Baillie,
" maketh wise men mad."

" What must it do then to men like us,
living as our fathers did a thousand years
since, and possessing scarce more lights
than they did ?—Can we view their bluidy
edicts against us—their hanging, heading,

1

hounding, and hunting down an ancient and honourable name, as deserving better treatment than that which enemies give to enemies?—Here I stand, have been in twenty frays, and never hurt man but when I was in het bluid; and yet they wad betray me and hang me like a masterless dog, at the gate of ony great man that has an ill will at me."

I replied, " that the proscription of his name and family sounded in English ears as a very cruel and arbitrary law;" and having thus far soothed him, I resumed my propositions of obtaining military employment for himself, if he chose it, and his sons in foreign parts. MacGregor shook me very cordially by the hand, and detaining me, so as to permit Mr Jarvie to precede us, a manœuvre for which the narrowness of the road served as an excuse, he said to me, " You are a kindhearted and an honourable youth, and understand, doubtless, that which is due to the feelings of a man of honour.—But the

heather that I have trod upon when living,
must bloom ower me when I am dead—my
heart would sink, and my arm would shrink
and wither like fern in the frost, were I to
lose sight of my native hills; nor has the
world a scene that would console me for
the loss of the rocks and cairns, wild as
they are, that you see around us.—And
Helen—what could become of her, were I
to leave her the subject of new insult and
atrocity?—or how could she bear to be removed from these scenes, where the remembrance of her wrongs is aye sweetened by
the recollection of her revenge?—I was
once so hard put at by my Great enemy,
as I may well ca' him, that I was forced
e'en to gie way to the tide, and removed
myself and my people and family from our
dwellings in our native land, and to with-
draw for a time into MacCallummore's
country—and Helen made a Lament on
our departure, as weel as MacRimmon
himsell could hae framed it—and so pite-

ously sad and waesome, that our hearts amaist broke as we sate and listened to her—it was like the wailing of one that mourns for the mother that bore him—the tears came down the rough faces of our gillies as they hearkened—and I wad not have the same touch of heartbreak again, no, not to have all the lands that ever were owned by MacGregor." *

" But your sons," I said, " they are at the age when your countrymen have usually no objection to see the world."

" And I should be content," he replied, " that they pushed their fortune in the French or Spanish service, as is the wont of Scottish cavaliers of honour, and last night your plan seemed feasible enough— But I hae seen his Excellency this morning before ye were up."

---

* This Lament is said still to be preserved, a circumstance which cannot fail to give authenticity to these Memoirs.—EDITOR.

"Did he then quarter so near us?" said I, my bosom throbbing with anxiety.

"Nearer than ye thought," was the reply; "but he seemed rather in some shape to jalouse your speaking to the young leddy, and so you see"——

"There was no occasion for jealousy," I answered, with some haughtiness; "I should not have intruded on his privacy."

"But ye must not be offended, or look out from amang your curls then, like a wild cat out of an ivy-tod, for ye are to understand that he wishes most sincere weel to ye, and has proved it. And it's partly that whilk has set the heather on fire e'en now."

"Heather on fire?" said I. "I do not understand you."

"Why," resumed MacGregor, "ye ken weel aneugh that women and gear are at the bottom of a' the mischief in this warld —I hae been misdoubting your cousin Rashleigh since ever he saw that he wasna to get Die Vernon for his marrow, and I

think he took grudge at his Excellency
mainly on that account. But then came
the splore about the surrendering your papers —and we hae now gude evidence,
that, sae sune as he was compelled to yield
them up, he rade post to Stirling; and
tauld the government all, and mair than
all, that was gaun dousely on amang us hill-
folk ; and, doubtless, that was the way that
the country was laid to take his Excellency and the leddy, and to make sic an unexpected raid on me. And I hae as little
doubt that the puir deevil Morris, whom
he could gar believe ony thing, was egg-
ed on by him, and some of the Lowland
gentry, to trepan me in the gate he tried
to do—But if Rashleigh Osbaldistone were
baith the last and best of his name; and
granting that he and I ever forgether again,
the fiend go down my weasand with a bare
blade at his belt, if we part before my dirk
and his best bluid are weel acquaint thegither."

He pronounced the last threat with an

ominous frown, and the appropriate gesture of his hand upon his dagger.

" I should almost rejoice at what has happened," said I, " could I hope that Rashleigh's treachery might prove the means of preventing the explosion of the rash and desperate intrigues, in which I have long suspected him to be a prime agent."

" Trow na ye that," said Rob Roy; " traitor's word never yet hurt honest cause. He was ower deep in our secrets, that's true, and had it not been so, Stirling and Edinburgh Castles would have been baith in our hands by this time, or briefly hereafter, whilk is now scarce to be hoped for. But there are ower mony engaged, and far ower gude a cause to be gi'en up for the breath of a traitor's tale, and that will be seen and heard of ere it be lang. And so, as I was about to say, the best of my thanks to you for your offer anent my sons, whilk last night I had some thoughts to have embraced in their behalf. But I see that this

villain's treason will convince our great
folks that they must instantly draw to a
head, and make a blow for it, or be ta'en
in their houses, coupled up like hounds,
and driven up to Lundin like the honest
noblemen and gentlemen in the year seventeen hundred and seven.   Civil war is like
a cockatrice ; we have sitten hatching the
egg that held it for ten years, and might
hae sitten on for ten years mair, when in
comes Rashleigh, and chips the shell, and
out bangs the wonder amang us, and cries
to fire and sword.   Now in sic a matter I'll
hae need o' a' the hands I can mak ; and,
nae disparagement to the Kings of France
and Spain, whom I wish very weel to,
King James is as guide a man as ony o'
them, and has the best right to Rob and
Hamish, being his natural-born subjects."

I easily comprehended that these words
boded a general national convulsion ; and,
as it would have been alike useless and
dangerous to have combatted the political
opinions of my guide, at such a place and

9

moment, I contented myself with regretting the promiscuous scene of confusion and distress likely to arise from any general exertion in favour of the exiled royal family.

" Let it come, man—let it come," answered MacGregor ; " ye never saw dull weather clear without a shower ; and if the world is turned upside down, why, honest men will have the better chance to cut bread out of it."

I again attempted to bring him back to the subject of Diana, but although on most occasions and subjects he used a freedom of speech which I had no great delight in listening to, yet upon that alone, which was most interesting to me, he kept a degree of scrupulous reserve, and contented himself with intimating, that he hoped " the leddy would be soon in a quieter country than this was like to be for one while." I was obliged to be content with this answer, and to proceed in the hope that accident might, as on a former occasion, stand my

friend, and allow me at least the sad grati-
fication of bidding farewell to the object who
had occupied such a share of my affections,
so much beyond even what I had supposed,
till I was about to be separated from her for
ever.

We pursued the margin of the lake for
about six English miles, through a devious
and beautifully variegated path, until we
attained a sort of Highland farm, or assem-
bly of hamlets, near the head of that fine
sheet of water, called, if I mistake not, Le-
diart, or some such name. Here a numerous party of MacGregor's men were stationed in order to receive us. The taste,
as well as the eloquence of tribes, in a
savage, or, to speak more properly, in a
rude state, is usually just, because it is un-
fettered by system and affectation, and of
this I had an example in the choice these
mountaineers had made of a place to receive their guests. It has been said that a
British monarch would judge well to receive the embassy of a rival power in the

cabin of a man-of-war; and a Highland leader acted with some propriety in chusing a situation where the natural objects of grandeur proper to his country might have the full effect on the mind of his guests.

We ascended about two hundred yards from the shores of the lake, guided by a brawling brook, and left on the right hand four or five Highland huts, with patches of arable land around them, cut as it were out of the surrounding copsewood, and waving with crops of barley and oats. Above this limited space the hill became more steep; and on its edge we descried the glittering arms and waving drapery of about fifty of MacGregor's followers. They were stationed on a spot, the recollection of which yet strikes me with admiration. The brook, hurling its waters downwards from the mountain, had in this spot encountered a barrier rock, over which it had made its way by two distinct leaps. The first fall, across which a magnificent old oak, slanting out from the farther bank, partly extended itself as if to shroud the dusky stream of the cascade, might be about twelve feet high; the broken waters were received in a beautiful stone bason, almost as regular as if hewn by a sculptor; and after wheeling around its flinty margin, they made a second precipitous dash through a dark and narrow chasm, at least fifty foot in depth, and from thence, in a hurried, but comparatively a more gentle course, escaped to join the lake.

With the natural taste which belongs to mountaineers, and especially to the Scottish Highlanders, whose feelings I have observed are often allied with the romantic and poetical, Rob Roy's wife and followers had prepared our morning repast in a scene well calculated to impress strangers with some feelings of awe. They are also naturally a grave and proud people; and, however rude in our estimation, carry their ideas of form and politeness to an excess that would appear overstrained, except

from the demonstration of superior force
which accompanies the display of it ; for it
must be granted that the air of punctilious
deference and rigid etiquette which would
seem ridiculous in an ordinary peasant,
has, like the salute of a *corps-de-garde*, a
propriety when tendered by a Highlander
completely armed.   There was, accordingly, a good deal of formality in our approach
and reception.

The Highlanders who had been dispersed on the side of the hill drew themselves
together when we came in view, and standing firm and motionless, appeared in close
column behind three figures whom I soon recognized to be Helen MacGregor and her
two sons. MacGregor himself arranged his
attendants in the rear, and requesting Mr
Jarvie to dismount where the ascent became steep, advanced slowly, marshalling
us forward at the head of the troop.   As
we advanced, we heard the wild notes of
the bagpipes, which lost their natural dis-
cord from being mingled with the dashing

sound of the cascade. When we came close, the wife of MacGregor came forward to meet us: Her dress was studiously arranged in a more feminine taste than it had been on the preceding day, but her features wore the same lofty, unbending, and resolute character; and as she folded my friend, the Baillie, in an unexpected and apparently unwelcome embrace, I could perceive, by the agitation of his wig, his back, and the calves of his legs, that he felt much like to one who feels himself suddenly in the gripe of a she bear, without being able to distinguish whether the animal is in kindness or in wrath. " Kinsman," she said, " you are welcome—and you too, stranger," she added, releasing my alarmed companion, who instinctively drew back and settled his wig, and addressing herself to me,—" You are also welcome—You came," she added, "to our unhappy country, when our bloods were chafed, and our hands were red. Excuse the rudeness that gave you a rough welcome, and lay it upon

the evil times, and not upon us." All this
was said with the manners of a princess,
and in the tone and style of a court. Nor
was there the least tincture of that vulga-
rity, which we naturally attach to the Lowland Scottish. There was a strong provin-
cial accentuation, but, otherwise, the language rendered by Helen MacGregor, out
of the native and poetical Gaelic, into English, which she had acquired as we do learned tongues, but had probably never heard
applied to the mean purposes of ordinary
life, was graceful, flowing, and declama-
tory. Her husband, who had in his time
played many parts, used a much less elevated and emphatic dialect,—but even *his*
language rose in purity of expression, as
you may have remarked, if I have been
accurate in recording it, when the affairs
which he discussed were of an agitating and
important nature; and it appears to me in
his case, and in that of some other Highlanders whom I have known, that when
familiar and facetious, they used the Low-

11

land Scottish dialect,—when serious and impassioned, their thoughts arranged themselves in the idiom of their native language; and in the latter case, as they uttered the corresponding ideas in English, the expressions sounded wild, elevated, and poetical. In fact, the language of passion is almost always pure as well as vehement, and it is no uncommon thing to hear a Scotchman, when overwhelmed by a countryman with a tone of bitter and fluent upbraiding, reply by way of taunt to his adversary, " You have gotten to your English."

Be this as it may, the wife of MacGregor invited us to a refreshment spread out on the grass, which abounded with all the good things their mountains could offer, but was clouded by the dark and undisturbed gravity which sat on the brow of our hostess, as well as by our deep and anxious recollection of what had taken place on the preceding day. It was in vain that the leader exerted himself to excite mirth : A chill hung over our minds as if the feast had been funereal; and every bosom felt light when it was ended.

"Adieu, cousin," she said to Mr Jarvie, as we arose from the entertainment; "the best wish Helen MacGregor can give to a friend is, that he may see her no more."

The Baillie struggled to answer, probably with some common-place maxim of morality; but the calm and melancholy sternness of her countenance bore down and disconcerted the mechanical and formal importance of the magistrate. He coughed,—hemmed,—bowed,—and was silent. "For you, stranger," she said, "I have a token from one whom you——

"Helen," interrupted MacGregor, in a loud and stern voice, "what means this,—have you forgotten the charge?"

"MacGregor," she replied, "I have forgotten nought that is fitting for me to remember. It is not such hands as these," and she stretched forth her long, sinewy, and bare arm, "that are fitted to convey love-tokens, were the gift connected with aught but misery.—Young man," she said, presenting me with a ring, which I well remembered as one of the few ornaments that Miss Vernon sometimes wore, " this comes from one whom you will never see more. If it is a joyless token, it is well fitted to pass through the hands of one to whom joy can never be known. Her last words were—Let him forget me for ever."

" And can she," I said, almost without being conscious that I spoke, " suppose that is possible ?"

" All may be forgotten," said the extraordinary female who addressed me,—" all —but the sense of dishonour, and the desire of vengeance."

" *Seid suas*," * cried the MacGregor, stamping with impatience. The bagpipes sounded, and, with their thrilling and jarring tones, cut short our conference. Our

---

* " Strike up."

leave of our hostess was taken by silent gestures; and we resumed our journey, with an additional proof on my part, that I was beloved by Diana, and was separated from her for ever.

CHAPTER IX.

Farewell to the land where the clouds love to rest,
Like the shroud of the dead, on the mountain's cold breast;
To the cataract's roar where the eagles reply,
And the lake her lone bosom expands to the sky.

Our route lay through a dreary, yet romantic country, which the distress of my
own mind prevented me from remarking
particularly, and which, therefore, I will
not attempt to describe. The lofty peak
of Ben Lomond, here the predominant
monarch of the mountains, lay on our
right hand, and served as a striking land-
mark. I was not awakened from my apathy, until, after a long and toilsome walk,
we emerged through a pass in the hills,
and Loch Lomond opened before us. I
will spare you the attempt to describe

L 2

what you will hardly comprehend without going to see it. But certainly this noble lake, boasting innumerable beautiful islands of every varying form and outline which fancy can form,—its northern extremity narrowing until it is lost among dusky and retreating mountains,—while, gradually widening as it extends to the southward, it spreads its base around the indentures and promontories of a fair and fertile land, affords one of the most surprising, beautiful, and sublime spectacles in nature. The eastern side, peculiarly rough and rugged, was at this time the chief seat of MacGregor and his clan, to curb whom a small garrison had been stationed in a central position betwixt Loch Lomond and another lake. The extreme strength of the country, however, with the numerous passes, marshes, caverns, and other places of concealment or defence, made the establishment of this little fort seem rather an acknowledgment of the danger, than an effectual means of securing against it.

Upon more than one occasion, as well as on that which I witnessed, the garrison suffered from the adventurous spirit of the outlaw and his followers. These advantages were never sullied by ferocity when he himself was in command ; for, equally good-tempered and sagacious, he understood well the danger of incurring unnecessary odium. I understood with pleasure that he had caused the captives of the preceding day to be liberated in safety ; and many traits of mercy, and even generosity, are recorded of this remarkable man on similar occasions.

A boat waited for us in a creek beneath a huge rock, manned by four lusty Highland rowers ; and our host took leave of us with great cordiality, and even affection. Betwixt him and Mr Jarvie, indeed, there seemed to exist a degree of mutual regard, which formed a strong contrast to their different occupations and habits. After kissing each other very lovingly, and when they were just in the act of parting, the

Baillie, in the fullness of his heart, and with a faultering voice, assured his kinsman, " that if ever an hundred pund, or even twa hundred, would put him or his family in a settled way, he need but just send a line to the Saut-Market ;" and Rob, grasping his basket-hilt with one hand, and shaking Mr Jarvie's heartily with the other, protested, " that if ever any body should affront his kinsman, an' he would but let him ken, he would stow his lugs out of his head, were he the best man in Glasgow."

With these assurances of mutual aid and continued good-will, we bore away from the shore, and took our course for the south-western angle of the lake, where it gives birth to the river Leven. Rob Roy remained for some time standing on the rock from beneath which we had departed, conspicuous by his long gun, waving tartans, and the single plume in his cap, which in those days denoted the Highland gentleman and soldier ; although I observe the present military taste has decorated the

Highland bonnet with a quantity of black plumage, resembling that which is borne before funerals. At length, as the distance increased between us, we saw him turn and go slowly up the side of the hill, followed by his immediate attendants or body guard.

We performed our voyage for a long time in silence, interrupted only by the Gaelic chaunt which one of the rowers sung in low irregular measure, rising occasionally into a wild chorus, in which the others joined.

My own thoughts were sad enough ; yet I felt something soothing in the magnificent scenery with which I was surrounded ; and thought, in the enthusiasm of the moment, that had my faith been that of Rome, I could have consented to live and die a lonely hermit in one of the romantic and beautiful islands amongst which our boat glided.

The Baillie had also his speculations,

but they were of somewhat a different
complexion ; as I found when, after about
an hour's silence, during which he had
been mentally engaged in the calculations
necessary, he undertook to prove the possibility of draining the lake, and " giving
to plough and harrow many hundred, ay,
many a thousand of acres, from whilk no
man could get earthly gude e'enow, unless
it were a gedd or a dish of perch now and
then."

Amidst a long discussion, which he
" crammed into mine ear against the stomach of my sense," I only remember, that
it was part of his project to preserve a portion of the lake just deep enough and broad
enough for the purposes of water-carriage,
so that coal barges and gabbards should
pass as easily between Dunbarton and Glenfalloch as between Glasgow and Greenock.

At length we neared our distinct place
of landing, adjoining to the ruins of an ancient castle, and just where the lake dis-

charges its superfluous waters into the Leven. There we found Dougal with the horses. The Baillie had formed a plan with respect to " the creature," as well as upon the draining of the Lake ; and, perhaps in both cases, with more regard to the utility than to the practical possibility of his scheme. " Dougal," he said, " ye are a kindly creature, and hae the sense and feeling o' what is due to your betters—and I'm e'en wae for you, Dougal, for it canna be but that in the life ye lead you suld get a Jeddart cast ae day, suner or later. I trust, considering my services as a magistrate, and my father the deacon afore me, I hae interest eneugh in the council to gar them wink awee at a waur faut than yours. Sae I hae been thinking that if ye will gang back to Glasgow wi' us, being a strong-backit creature, ye might be employed in the ware-house till something better suld cast up."

" Her nainsel muckle obliged till the Baillie's honour," replied Dougal ; " but teil be in her shanks fan she gangs on a causeway'd street, unless she be drawn up the Gallowgate wi' tows as she was before."

In fact, I afterwards learned that Dougal had originally come to Glasgow as a prisoner, from being concerned in some depredation, but had some how found such favour in the eyes of the jailor, that, with rather over-weening confidence, he had retained him in his service as one of the turnkeys; a task which Dougal had discharged with sufficient fidelity, so far as was known, until overcome by his clannish prejudices on the unexpected appearance of his old leader.

Astonished at receiving so round a refusal to so favourable an offer, the Baillie, turning to me, observed, that the " creature was a natural born ideot." I testified my own gratitude in a way which Dougal much better relished, by slipping a couple of guineas into his hands. He no sooner felt the touch of the gold, than he sprung twice or thrice from the earth with the agility of a wild buck, flinging out first one heel and

then another, in a manner which would
have astonished a French dancing-master.
He ran to the boatmen to shew them the
prize, and a small gratuity made them take
part in his raptures. He then, to use a
favourite expression of the dramatic John
Bunyan, " went on his way, and I saw
him no more."

The Baillie and I mounted our horses,
and proceeded on the road to Glasgow.
When we had lost the view of the lake, and
its superb amphitheatre of mountains, I
could not help expressing, with enthusiasm,
my sense of its natural beauties, although I
was conscious that Mr Jarvie was a very un-
congenial spirit to communicate with on
such a subject.

" Ye are a young gentleman," he replied,
" and an Englishman, and a' this may be
very fine to you; but for me, who am a
plain man, and ken something o' the different values of land, I wad nae gie the
finest sight we hae seen in the Hielands,
for the first keek o' the Gorbals o' Glas-

gow; and if I were ance there, it suldna be every fule's errand, begging your pardon, Mr Francis, that suld take me out o' sight o' Saint Mungo's steeple again!"

The honest man had his wish; for, by dint of travelling very late, we arrived at his own house that night, or rather on the succeeding morning. Having seen my worthy fellow-traveller safely consigned to the charge of the considerate and officious Mattie, I proceeded to Mrs Flyter's, in whose house, even at this unwonted hour, light was still burning. The door was opened by no less a person than Andrew Fairservice himself, who, upon the first sound of my voice, set up a loud shout of joyful recognition, and, without uttering a syllable, ran up stairs towards a parlour on the second floor, from the windows of which the light proceeded. Justly conceiving that he went to announce my return to the anxious Owen, I followed him upon the foot. Owen was not alone,—there was another in the apartment,—it was my father.

The first impulse was to preserve the dignity of his usual equanimity,—" Francis, I am glad to see you."—The next was to embrace me tenderly,—" My dear—dear son."—Owen secured one of my hands, and wetted it with his tears, while he joined in gratulating my return. These are scenes which address themselves to the eye and to the heart, rather than to the ear.—My old eye-lids still moisten at the recollection of our meeting; but your kind and affectionate feelings can well imagine what I should find it impossible to describe.

When the tumult of our joy was over, I learned that my father had arrived from Holland shortly after Owen had set off for Scotland. Determined and hasty in all his movements, he only stopped to provide the means of discharging the obligations incumbent on his house. By his extensive resources, with funds enlarged, and credit fortified, by eminent success in his continental speculation, he easily accomplished what perhaps his absence alone rendered difficult, and set out for Scotland to exact justice from Rashleigh Osbaldistone, as well as to put order to his affairs in that country. My father's arrival in full credit, and with the ample means of supporting his engagements honourably, as well as benefitting his correspondents in future, was a stunning blow to MacVittie and Company, who had conceived his star set for ever. Highly incensed at the usage his confidential clerk and agent had received at their hands, Mr Osbaldistone refused every tender of apology and accommodation ; and, having settled the balance of their account, announced to them, that with all its numerous contingent advantages, that leaf of their ledger was closed for ever.

While he enjoyed this triumph over false friends, he was not a little alarmed on my account. Owen, good man, had not supposed it possible that a journey of fifty or sixty miles, which may be made with so much ease and safety in any direction from London, could be attended with

any particular danger. But he caught
alarm, by sympathy, from my father, to
whom the country, and the lawless character of its inhabitants, were better known.

These apprehensions were raised to agony, when, a few hours before I arrived,
Andrew Fairservice made his appearance,
with a dismal and exaggerated account of
the uncertain state in which he had left
me. The nobleman with whose troops he
had been a sort of prisoner, had, after examination, not only dismissed him, but furnished him with the means of returning
rapidly to Glasgow, in order to announce
to my friends my precarious and unpleasant
situation.

Andrew was one of those persons who
have no objection to the sort of temporary attention and woeful importance
which attaches itself to the bearer of bad
tidings, and had therefore by no means
smoothed down his tale in the telling, especially as the rich London merchant himself proved unexpectedly one of the audi-

tors. He went at great length into an account of the dangers I had escaped, chiefly, as he insinuated, by means of his own experience, exertion, and sagacity.

" What was to come of me now, when my better angel, in his (Andrew's) person, was removed from my side, it was," he said, " sad and sair to conjecture ; but the Baillie was nae better than just naebody at a pinch, or something waur, for he was a conceited body, and Andrew hated conceit—but certainly atween the pistols and the carabines of the troopers that rappit aff the tane after the tother as fast as hail, and the dirks and claymores o' the Hielanders, and the deep waters and weils o' the Avondow, it was to be thought there wad be a puir account of the young gentleman."

‹ This statement would have driven Owen to despair, had he been alone and unsupported ; but my father's perfect knowledge of mankind enabled him easily to appreciate the character of Andrew, and the real amount of his intelligence. Stripped of all exaggeration, however, it was alarming enough to a parent. He determined to set out in person to obtain my liberty, by ransom or negociation, and was busied with Owen till a late hour, in order to get through some necessary correspondence, and devolve on the latter some business which should be transacted during his absence, and thus it chanced that I found them watchers.

It was late ere we separated to our rest, and, too impatient long to endure repose, I was stirring early the next morning. Andrew gave his attendance at my levee, as in duty bound, and, instead of the scarecrow figure to which he had been reduced at Aberfoil, now appeared in the attire of an undertaker, a goodly suit, namely, of the deepest mourning. It was not till after one or two queries, which the rascal affected as long as he could to misunderstand, that I found out he " had thought it but decent to put on mourning, on account of my inexpressible loss ; and as the broker at whose shop he had equipped himself, declined to receive the goods again, and as his own garments had been destroyed or carried off in my honour's service, doubtless I' and my honourable father, whom Providence had blessed wi' the means, wadna suffer a puir lad to sit down wi' the loss; a stand o' claes was nae great matter to an Osbaldistone (be praised for't!) especially to an auld and attached servant o' the house."

As there was something of justice in Andrew's plea of loss in my service, his finesse succeeded; and he came by a good suit of mourning, with a beaver and all things conforming, as the exterior signs of woe for a master who was alive and merry.

My father's first care, when he arose, was to visit Mr Jarvie, for whose kindness he entertained the most grateful sentiments, which he expressed in very few but manly and nervous terms. He explained the altered state of his affairs, and offered the Baillie, on such terms as could not but be both advantageous and acceptable, that part in his concerns which had been hitherto managed by MacVittie and Company. The Baillie heartily congratulated my father and Owen on the changed posture of their affairs, and, without affecting to disclaim that he had done his best to serve them, when matters looked otherwise, he said, " He had only just acted as he wad be dune by—that, as to the extension of their correspondence, he frankly accepted it with thanks. Had MacVittie's folk behaved like honest men," he said, " he wad hae liked ill to hae come in ahint them, and out afore them, this gate. But it's otherwise, and they maun e'en stand the loss."

The Baillie then pulled me by the sleeve into a corner, and after again cordially wishing me joy, proceeded in rather an embarrassed tone.

" I wad heartily wish, Maister Francis, there suld be as little said as possible about the queer things we saw up yonder awa— There's nae gude, unless ane were judicially examinate, to say ony thing about that awfu' job o' Morris—and the members o' the council wadna think it creditable in ane of their body to be fighting wi' a wheen Hielandmen, and singeing their plaidens— And abune a', though I am a decent sponsible man, when I am on my right end, I canna but think I maun hae made a queer figure without my hat and my periwig, hinging by the middle like bawdrons, or a cloak flung ower a cloak-pin. Baillie Grahame wad hae an unco hair in my neck an' he got that tale by the end."

I could not suppress a smile when I recollected the Baillie's situation, although I certainly thought it no laughing matter at the time. The good-natured merchant was a little confused, but smiled also when he shook his head. "I see how it is—I see how it is. But say naething about it— there's a gude callant; and charge that lang-tongued, conceited, upsetting, serving-man o' yours, to say naething neither. I wadna for ever sae muckle that even the

lassock Mattie kenn'd ony thing about it.
I wad never hear an end o't."

He was obviously relieved from his im-
pending fears of ridicule, when I told him
it was my father's intention to leave Glasgow almost immediately. Indeed he had
now no motive for remaining, since the
most valuable part of the papers carried
off by Rashleigh had been recovered. For
that portion which he had converted into
cash and expended in his own or on political intrigue, there was no mode of recovering it but by a suit at law, which was forth-
with commenced, and proceeded, as our
law-agents assured us, with all deliberate
speed.

We spent, accordingly, one hospitable
day with the Baillie, and took leave of
him, as this narrative now does. He continued to grow in wealth, honour, and credit, and actually rose to the highest civic
honours in his native city. About two
years after the period I have mentioned,
he tired of his bachelor life, and promo-

ted Mattie from her wheel by the kitchen fire, to the upper end of his table, in the character of Mrs Jarvie. Baillie Grahame, the MacVitties, and others, (for all men have their enemies, especially in the council of a royal burgh,) ridiculed this transformation. " But," said Mr Jarvie, " let them say their say. I'll ne'er fash mysell, nor lose my liking for sae feckless a matter as a nine days' clash. My honest father the deacon had a byeword,

> ' Brent brow and lily skin,
> A loving heart, and a leal within,
> Is better than gowd or gentle kin.'

Besides," as he always concluded, " Mattie was nae ordinary lassock-quean ; she was akin to the Laird o' Limmerfield."

Whether it was owing to her descent or her gude gifts, I do not presume to decide ; but Mattie behaved excellently in her exaltation, and relieved the apprehensions of some of the Baillie's friends, who had deemed his experiment somewhat hazardous. I

do not know that there was any other inci-
dent of his quiet and useful life worthy of
being particularly recorded.

CHAPTER X.

"Come ye hither, my 'six' good sons,
   Gallant men I trowe ye be,
How many of you, my children dear,
   Will stand by that good Earl and me?"

"'Five' of them did answer make—
   'Five' of them spoke hastilie,
'O father, till the day we die,
   We'll stand by that good Earl and thee.'"
         The Rising in the North.

ON the morning when we were to depart
from Glasgow, Andrew Fairservice bounced
into my apartment like a madman, jumping
up and down, and singing, with more vehemence than tune,

The kiln's on fire—the kiln's on fire—
The kiln's on fire—she's a' in a lowe.

With some difficulty I prevailed on him to cease his confounded clamour, and explain to me what the matter was. He was pleased to inform me, as if he had been bringing the finest news imaginable, " that the Hielands were clean broken out every man o' them, and that Rob Roy, and a' his breekless bands, wad be down upon Glasgow, or twenty-four hours o' the clock gaed round."

" Hold your tongue," said I, " you scoundrel! You must be drunk or mad ; and if there is any truth in your news, is it a singing matter, you blockhead ?"

" Drunk or mad ? nae-doubt," replied Andrew, dauntlessly ; " ane's ay drunk or mad if he tells what grit folks dinna like to hear—Sing ? odd, the clans will make us sing on the wrang side o' our mouth, if we are sae drunk or mad as to bide their coming."

I rose in great haste, and I found my father and Owen also on foot, and in considerable alarm.

Andrew's news proved but too true in

the main. The great rebellion which agitated Britain in the year 1715 had already
broken out, by the unfortunate Earl of
Marr's setting up the standard of the Stuart
family in an ill-omened hour, to the ruin
of many honourable families, both in England and Scotland. The treachery of some
of the jacobite agents, (Rashleigh amongst
the rest,) and the arrest of others, had
made George the First's government acquainted with the extensive ramifications
of a conspiracy long prepared, and which
at last exploded prematurely, and in a part
of the kingdom too distant to have any vi-
tal effect upon the country, which, however,
was plunged into great confusion.

This great public event served to con-
firm and elucidate the obscure explanations
I had received from MacGregor; and I
could easily see why the westland clans,
who were brought against him, should
have waived their private quarrel, in consideration that they were all shortly to be
engaged in the same public cause. It was

a more melancholy reflection to my mind,
that Diana Vernon was the wife of one of
those who were most active in turning the
world upside down, and that she was herself exposed to all the privations and perils
of her husband's hazardous trade.

We held an immediate consultation on
the measures we were to adopt in this crisis, and acquiesced in my father's plan,
that we should instantly get the necessary
passports, and make the best of our way
to London. I acquainted my father with
my wish to offer my personal service to
the government in any volunteer corps, of
which several were already spoken of. He
readily acquiesced in my proposal; for,
though he disliked war as a profession
upon principle, no man would have exposed his life more willingly in defence of
civil and religious liberty.

We travelled in haste and in peril through
Dumfries-shire and the neighbouring coun-
ties of England. In this quarter, gentle-

men of the Tory interest were already in
motion mustering men and horses, while
the Whigs assembled themselves in the
principal towns, armed the inhabitants, and
prepared for civil war. We narrowly escaped being stopped upon more occasions
than one, and were often compelled to
take circuitous routes to avoid the points
where forces were assembling.

When we reached London, we immediately associated with those bankers and
eminent merchants who agreed to support
the credit of government, and to meet that
run upon the Funds, upon which the conspirators had greatly founded their hopes
of furthering their undertaking, by rendering the government, as it were, bankrupt.
My father was chosen one of the members
of this formidable body of the monied interest, as all had the greatest confidence in
his zeal, skill, and activity. He was also
the organ by which they communicated
with government, and contrived, from funds
belonging to his own house, or over which

he had command, to find purchasers for a quantity of the national stock, which was suddenly flung into the market at a depreciated price when the rebellion broke out. I was not idle myself, but obtained a commission, and levied, at my father's expence, about two hundred men, with whom I joined General Carpenter's army.

The rebellion, in the mean time, had extended itself to England. The unfortunate Earl of Derwentwater had taken arms in the cause, along with General Foster. My poor uncle, Sir Hildebrand, whose estate was reduced to almost nothing by his own carelessness and the expence and debauchery of his sons and household, was easily persuaded to join that unfortunate standard. Before doing so, however, he exhibited a degree of precaution of which no one could have suspected him—he made his will!

By this document he devised his estates of Osbaldistone-Hall, and so forth, to his sons successively, and their male heirs, until

he came to Rashleigh, whom, on account
of the turn he had lately taken in poli-
tics, he detested with all his might,—he
cut him with a shilling, and settled the
estate on me, as his next heir. I had always been rather a favourite of the old gentleman ; but it is probable that, confident
in the number of gigantic youths who now
armed around him, he considered the destination as likely to remain a dead letter,
which he inserted chiefly to show his dis-
pleasure at Rashleigh's treachery, both
public and domestic. There was an arti-
cle, by which he bequeathed to the niece
of his late wife, Diana Vernon, now Lady
Diana Vernon Beauchamp, some diamonds
belonging to her late aunt, and a great silver ewer, having the arms of Vernon and
Osbaldistone quarterly engraven upon it.

But Heaven had decreed a more speedy
extinction of his numerous and healthy li-
neage than, most probably, he himself had
reckoned on. In the very first muster of
the conspirators at a place called Green-

Rigg, Thorncliffe Osbaldistone quarrelled about precedence with a gentleman of the Northumbrian border, to the full as fierce and intractable as himself. In spite of all remonstrances, they gave their commander a specimen of how far their discipline might be relied upon, by fighting it out with their rapiers, and my kinsman was killed on the spot. His death was a great loss to Sir Hildebrand, for, notwithstanding his infernal temper, he had a grain or two of more sense than belonged to the rest of the brotherhood, Rashleigh always excepted.

Perceval, the sot, died also in his calling. He had a wager with another gentleman, who, from his exploits in that line, had acquired the formidable epithet of Brandy Swalewell, which should drink the largest cup of strong liquor when King James was proclaimed by the insurgents at Morpeth. The exploit was something enormous. I forget the exact quantity of brandy which Percie swallowed, but it oc-

10

casioned a fever, of which he expired at the end of three days, with the word, *water*, *water*, perpetually on his tongue. ·

, Dickon broke his neck near Warrington Bridge, in an attempt to show off a foundered blood-mare, which he wished to palm upon a Manchester merchant who had joined the insurgents. He pushed the animal at a five-barred gate; she fell in the leap, and the unfortunate jockey lost his life.

Wilfred the fool, as sometimes befalls, had the best fortune of the family. He was slain at Proud Preston, in Lancashire, on the day that General Carpenter attack-.ed the barricades, fighting with great bra-very, though I have heard he was never able exactly to comprehend the cause of quarrel, and did not uniformly remember on which king's side he was engaged. John also behaved very boldly in the same engagement, and received several wounds, of which he was not happy enough to die on the spot.

Old Sir Hildebrand, entirely broken-hearted by these successive losses, became, by the next day's surrender, one of the unhappy prisoners, and was lodged in Newgate with his wounded son John.

I was now released from my military duty, and lost no time therefore in endeavouring to relieve the distresses of these near relations. My father's interest with government, and the general compassion excited by a parent who had sustained the successive loss of so many sons within so short a time, would have prevented my uncle and cousin from being brought to trial for high treason; but their doom was given forth from a greater tribunal. John died of his wounds in Newgate, recommending to me, with his last breath, a cast of hawks which he had at the Hall, and a black spaniel bitch, called Lucy.

My poor uncle seemed beaten down to the very earth by his family calamities, and the circumstances in which he unexpectedly found himself. He said little; but seemed grateful for such attentions as circumstances permitted me to show him. I did not witness his meeting with my father for the first time for so many years, and under circumstances so melancholy; but judging from my father's extreme depression of spirits, it must have been melancholy in the last degree. Sir Hildebrand spoke with great bitterness against Rashleigh, now his only surviving child; laid upon him the ruin of his house, and the deaths of all his brethren, and declared, that neither he nor they would have plunged into political intrigue, but for that very member of his family who had been the first to desert them. He once or twice mentioned Diana, always with great affection; and once he said, while I sate by his bedside—"Nevoy, since Thorncliffe and all of them are dead, I am sorry you cannot have her."

The expression affected me much at the time; for it was a usual expression of the poor old Baronet's, when joyously setting forth upon the morning's chase, to distinguish Thorncliffe, who was a favourite, while he summoned the rest more generally; and

the loud jolly tone in which he used to hollo,
" Call Thornie—call all of them," contrasted sadly with the woe-begone and self-aban-
doning note in which he uttered the discon-
solate words which I have above quoted.
He mentioned the contents of his will, and
supplied me with an authenticated copy—
the original he had deposited with my old
acquaintance Mr Justice Inglewood, who,
dreaded by no one, and confided in by all
as a kind of neutral person, had become,
for aught I know, the depositary of half the
wills of those of both sides in the county of
Northumberland.

The greater part of my uncle's last hours
were spent in the discharge of the religious
duties of his church, in which he was directed by the chaplain of the Sardinian ambassador, for whom, with some difficulty, we
obtained permission to visit him.   I could
not ascertain by my own observation, or
through the medical attendants, that Sir Hildebrand Osbaldistone died of any formed
complaint bearing a name in the science of

medicine. He seemed to me completely worn out and broken down by fatigue of body and distress of mind, and rather cea-sed to exist than died of any positive strug-gle; just as a vessel, buffetted and tossed by a succession of tempestuous gales, her tim-bers overstrained, and her joints loosened, will sometimes spring a leak and founder, when there are no apparent causes for her destruction.

It was a remarkable circumstance, that my father, after the last duties were be-queathed to his brother, appeared suddenly to imbibe a strong anxiety that I should act upon the will, and represent his father's house, which had hitherto seemed to be the thing in the world which had least charms for him. But formerly, he had been only like the fox in the fable, contemning what was beyond his reach; and, moreover, I doubt not that the excessive dislike which he entertained against Rashleigh (now Sir Rashleigh) Osbaldistone, who loudly threatened to attack his father Sir Hildebrand's will and settlement, corroborated my father's desire to maintain it.

" He had been most unjustly disinherited," he said, " by his own father—his brother's will had repaired the disgrace, if not the injury, by leaving the wreck of the property to Frank, the natural heir, and he was determined the bequest should take effect."

In the meantime, Rashleigh was not altogether a contemptible personage as an opponent. The information he had given to government was critically well-timed, and his extreme plausibility, with the extent of his information, and the artful manner in which he contrived to assume both merit and influence, had, to a certain extent, procured him patrons among the ministers. We were already in the full tide of litigation with him on the subject of his pillaging the firm of Osbaldistone and Tresham ; and, judging from the progress

we made in that comparatively simple law-
suit, there was a chance that this second
course of litigation might be drawn out
beyond the period of all our natural lives.

· To avert these delays as much as possible, my father, by the advice of his counsel learned in the law, paid off and vested
in my person the rights to certain large
mortgages, affecting Osbaldistone - Hall.
Perhaps, however, the opportunity to con-
vert a great share of the large profits which
accrued from the rapid rise of the funds
upon the suppression of the rebellion, and
the experience he had so lately of the perils of commerce, encouraged him to rea-
lize, in this manner, a considerable part of
his property. At any rate, it so chanced,
that, instead of commanding me to the
desk, as I fully expected, having intimated
my willingness to comply with his wishes,
however they might destine me, I received
his directions to go down to Osbaldistone-
Hall, and take possession of it as the heir

and representative of the family. I was directed to apply to Squire Inglewood for the copy of my uncle's will deposited with him, and take all necessary measures to secure that possession, which sages say makes nine points of the law.

At another time I should have been delighted with this change of destination. But now Osbaldistone Hall was accompanied with many painful recollections. Still, however, I thought that in that neighbourhood only I was likely to acquire some information respecting the fate of Diana Vernon. I had every reason to fear it must be far different from what I could have wished it. But I could obtain no light upon her fate. It was in vain that I endeavoured, by such acts of kindness as their situation admitted, to conciliate the confidence of some distant relations who were among the prisoners in Newgate. A pride which I could not condemn, and a natural suspicion of the Whig, Frank Os-

báldistone, cousin to the double-distilled
traitor, Rashleigh, closed every heart and
tongue, and I only received thanks, cold
and extorted, in exchange for such benefits as I had power to offer. The arm
of the law was also gradually abridging
the numbers of those whom I endeavoured
to serve, and the hearts of the survivors
became gradually more contracted towards
all whom they conceived to be concerned
with the existing government. As they
were led gradually, and by detachments,
to execution, those who survived lost interest in mankind, and the desire of communicating with them. I shall long remember that one of them, Ned Shafton by
name, replied to my anxious enquiry, whether there was any indulgence I could procure him? " Mr Frank Osbaldistone, I
must suppose you mean me kindly, and
therefore I thank you.—But, by G—, men
cannot be fattened.like poultry, when they
see their neighbours carried off day by day

to the place of execution, and know that their own necks are to be twisted in their turn."

Upon the whole, therefore, I was glad to escape from London, from Newgate, and from the scenes which both exhibited, to breathe the free air of Northumberland. Andrew Fairservice had continued in my service more from my father's pleasure than my own. At present there seemed a prospect that his local acquaintance with Osbaldistone-Hall and its vicinity might be useful; and, of course, he accompanied me on my journey, and I enjoyed the prospect of getting rid of him, by establishing him in his old quarters. I cannot conceive how he could prevail upon my father to interest himself in him, unless it were by the art, which he possessed in no inconsiderable degree, of affecting an extreme attachment to his master, which theoretical attachment he made compatible in practice with playing all manner of tricks without scruple, providing only against his

master being cheated by any one but himself.

We performed our journey to the North
without any remarkable adventure, and we
found the country, so lately agitated by rebellion, now peaceful and in good order.
The more near we approached to Osbaldistone-Hall, the more did my heart sink at
the thought of entering that deserted mansion, until, in order to postpone the evil
day, I resolved first to make my visit at Mr
Justice Inglewood's.

That venerable person had been much
disturbed with thoughts of what he had
been, and what he now was; and natural
recollections of the past had interfered con-
siderably with the active duty, which, in
his present situation, might have been expected from him. He was fortunate, however, in one respect : He had got rid of his
clerk Jobson, who had finally left him in
dudgeon at his inactivity, and become legal assistant to a certain Squire Standish,

who had lately commenced operations in these parts as a justice, with a zeal for King George and the Protestant succession, which, very different from the feelings of his old patron, Mr Jobson had more occasion to restrain within the bounds of the law, than to stimulate to exertion.

Old Justice Inglewood received me with great courtesy, and readily exhibited my uncle's will, which seemed to be without a flaw. He was for some time in obvious distress, how he should speak and act in my presence; but when he found, that though a supporter of the present government upon principle, I was disposed to think with pity on those who had opposed it on a mistaken feeling of loyalty and duty, his discourse became a very diverting medley of what he had done, and what he had left undone,—the pains he had taken to prevent some squires from joining, and to wink at the escape of others, who had been so unlucky as to engage in the affair.

We were *tete-a-tete*, and several bumpers had been quaffed by the Justice's special desire, when, on a sudden, he requested me to fill a *bona fide* brimmer to the health of poor dear Die Vernon, the rose of the wilderness,—the heath-bell of Cheviot, and the blossom that's transplanted to a damned convent.

" Is not Miss Vernon married then ?" I exclaimed, in great astonishment. "I thought his Excellency"——

" Pooh ! pooh ! his Excellency and his Lordship's all a humbug now, you know—mere St Germain titles—earl of Beauchamp, and ambassador plenipotentiary from France, when the Duke Regent of Orleans scarce knew that he lived, I dare say. But you must have seen old Sir Frederick Vernon at the Hall, when he played the part of Father Vaughan."

" Good Heavens ! then Vaughan was Miss Vernon's father !"

" To be sure he was," said the Justice, coolly ; " there's no use in keeping the secret now, for he must be out of the country by this time—otherwise, no doubt, it would be my duty to apprehend him.— Come, off with your bumper to my dear lost Die,

And let her health go round, around, around,
　And let her health go round ;
For though your stocking be of silk,
　Your knees near kiss the ground, aground, aground."

I was unable, as the reader may easily conceive, to join in the Justice's jollity. My head swam with the shock I had received. " I never heard," I said, " that Miss Vernon's father was living."

" It was not our government's fault that he is," replied Inglewood ; " for the devil a man there is whose-head would have brought more money. He was condemned to death for Fenwick's plot, and was thought to have had some hand in the Knight-bridge affair, in King William's time; and as he had married in Scotland, to a relation of the house of Breadalbane, he pos-

sessed great influence with all their chiefs.
There was a talk of his being demanded to
be given up at the peace of Ryswick, but he
shammed ill, and his death was given pub-
licly out in the French papers.   But when
he came back here on the old score, we old
cavaliers knew him well, — that is to say, I
knew him, not as being a cavalier myself,
but no information being lodged against
the poor gentleman, and my memory being
shortened by frequent attacks of the gout,
I could not have sworn to him, you know."

"Was he then not known at Osbaldistone Hall?" I enquired.

"To none but to his daughter, the old
knight, and Rashleigh, who had got at that
secret as he did at every one else, and held
it like a twisted cord about poor Die's neck.
I have seen her one hundred times she would
have spit at him, if it had not been fear for
her father, whose life would not have been
worth five minutes purchase if he had been
discovered to the government—But don't
mistake me, Mr Osbaldistone; I say the go-

vernment is a good, a gracious, and a just government, and if it has hanged one half of the rebels, poor things, all will acknow. ledge they would not have been touched had they staid at home."

Waving the discussion of these political questions, I brought back Mr Inglewood to his subject, and I found that Diana, having positively refused to marry any of the Osbaldistone family, and expressed her particular detestation of Rashleigh, he had from that time begun to cool in zeal for the cause of the Pretender; to which, as the youngest of six brethren, bold, artful, and able, he had hitherto looked forward as the means of making his fortune. Probably the compulsion with which he had been forced to render up his ill-gotten spoils, by the united authority of Sir Frederick Vernon, and the Scottish Chiefs, had determined his resolution to make his fortune by changing his opinions, and betraying his trust. Perhaps also, for few men were better judges where his interest was concerned, he considered their means and talents to be, as they afterwards proved, greatly inadequate to the important task of overthrowing an established government. Sir Frederick Vernon, or, as he was called among the Jacobites, his Excellency Viscount Beauchamp, had, with his daughter, some difficulty in escaping the consequences of Rashleigh's information. Here Mr Inglewood's information was at fault; but he did not doubt, since we had not heard of Sir Frederick being in the hands of the government, he must be by this time abroad, where, agreeable to the cruel bond he had entered into with his brother-in-law, she must, since he had declined to select a husband out of the Osbaldistone family, be confined to a convent. The original cause of this singular agreement Mr Inglewood could not perfectly explain; but he understood it was a family compact, entered into for the purpose of securing to Sir Frederick the rents of the remnant of his large estates, which had been vested in the

Osbaldistone family by some legal manœuvre; in short, a family compact, in which,
like many of those undertaken at that time
of day, the feelings of the principal parties
interested were no more regarded than if
they had been a part of the live-stock upon
the lands.

I cannot tell, such is the waywardness
of the human heart, whether this intelligence gave me joy or sorrow. It seemed
to me, that, in the knowledge that Miss
Vernon was eternally divided from me,
not by marriage with another, but by seclusion in a convent, in order to fulfil an
absurd bargain of this kind, my regret for
her loss was aggravated rather than diminished. I became dull, low-spirited, absent, and unable to support the task of
conversing with Justice Inglewood, who
in his turn yawned, and proposed to retire
early. I took leave of him overnight, de-
termining the next day before breakfast, to
ride over to Osbaldistone-Hall.

Mr Inglewood acquiesced in my propo-

sal.   " It would be well," he said, " that I
made my appearance there before I was
known to be in the country, the more especially as Sir Rashleigh Osbaldistone was
now, he understood, at Mr Jobson's house,
hatching some mischief doubtless.—They
were fit company," he added, " for each
other, Sir Rashleigh having lost all right to
mingle in the society of men of honour ; but
it was hardly possible two such damned
rascals should collogue together without
mischief to honest people."

He concluded, by earnestly recommending a toast and tankard, and an attack upon his venison pasty, before I set out in
the morning, just to break the cold air on
the wolds.

CHAPTER XI.

His master's gone, and no one now
Dwells in the halls of Ivor;
Men, dogs, and horses all are dead,
He is the sole survivor.

                            . WORDSWORTH.

THERE are few more melancholy sensations than those with which we regard
scenes of past pleasure, when altered and
deserted. In my ride to Osbaldistone-Hall,
I past the same objects which I had seen
in company with Miss Vernon on the day
of our memorable ride from Inglewood
Place. Her spirit seemed to keep me company on the way; and, when I passed the
spot where I had first seen her, I almost
listened for the cry of the hounds and
the notes of the horn, and strained my eye·

N. 2

on vacant space, as if to descry the fair
huntress again descend like an apparition
from the hill.   But all was silent, and all
was solitary. When I reached the Hall, the
closed doors and windows, the grass-grown
pavement, the courts, which were now so
silent, presented a strong contrast to the
gay and bustling scene I had so often seen
them exhibit, when the merry hunters were
going forth to their morning sport, or returning.   The joyous bark of the fox-
hounds as they were uncoupled, the cries
of the huntsman, the clang of the horses'
hoof, the loud laugh of the old knight at
the head of his strong and numerous de-
scendants, were all silenced now and for
ever.

   While I gazed round the scene of solitude and emptiness, I was inexpressibly
affected, even by recollecting those whom,
when alone, I had no reason to regard
with affection.   But the thought that so
many youths of goodly presence, warm with
life, health, and confidence, were within so

short a time cold in the grave, by various
yet all violent and unexpected modes of
death, afforded a picture of mortality at
which the mind trembled. It was little
consolation to me that I returned a pro-
prietor to the halls, which I had left almost like a fugitive. My mind was not
habituated to regard the scenes around
as my property, and I felt myself like a
usurper, at least an intruding stranger, and
could hardly divest myself of the idea, that
some of the bulky forms of my deceased
kinsmen were, like the gigantic spectres of
a romance, to appear in the gateway, and
dispute my entrance.

While I was engaged in these sad
thoughts, my follower, Andrew, whose feelings were of a very different nature, exerted himself in thundering alternately on
every door in the building, calling, at the
same time, for admittance, in a tone so
loud as to intimate, that *he*, at least, was
fully sensible of his newly-acquired importance as squire of the body to the new lord-

of-the-manor. At length, timidly and reluctantly, Anthony Syddall, my uncle's
aged butler, and major-domo, presented
himself at a lower window, well fenced
with iron bars, and enquired our business.

" We are come to take your charge aff
your hand, my auld friend," said Andrew
Fairservice ; " ye may gie up your keys as
sune as ye like—ilka dog has his day. I'll
take the plate and napery aff your hand.
Ye hae had your ain time o't, Mr Syddall ;
but ilka bean has its black, and ilka path
has its puddle ; and it will just set you
henceforth to sit at the bcard-end, as weel
as it did Andrew lang syne."

Checking with some difficulty the for-
wardness of my follower, I explained to
Syddall the nature of my right, and the title I had to demand admittance into the
Hall, as into my own property. The old
man seemed much agitated and distressed,
and testified manifest reluctance to give me
entrance, although it was couched in a hum-
ble and submissive tone. I allowed for the

agitation of natural feelings, which really did the old man honour; but continued peremptory in my demand of admittance, explaining to him that his refusal would oblige me to apply for Mr Inglewood's warrant, and a constable.

" We are come from Mr Justice Inglewood's this morning," said Andrew, to enforce the menace, " and I saw Archie Rutledge, the constable, as I came up by— the country's no to be lawless as it has been, Mr Syddall, letting rebels and papists gang on as they best listed."

The threat of the law sounded dreadful in the old man's ears, conscious as he was of the suspicion under which he himself lay, from his religion and his devotion to Sir Hildebrand and his sons. He undid, with fear and trembling, one of the postern entrances, which was secured with many a bolt and bar, and humbly hoped that I would excuse him for fidelity in the discharge of his duty.—I reassured him, and

told him I had the better opinion of him
for his caution.

"Sae have not I," said Andrew; "Syddall is an auld sneck-drawer; he wadna be
looking as white as a sheet, and his knees
knocking thegether, unless it were for something mair than he's like to tell us."

" Lord forgive you, Mr Fairservice," replied the butler, " to say such things of an
old friend and fellow-servant !—Where"—
following me humbly along the passage,
" where would it be your honour's pleasure to have a fire lighted ? I fear me you
will find the house very dull and dreary—
But perhaps you ride back to Inglewood
Place to dinner ?"

" Light a fire in the library," replied I.

" In the library !"—answered the old man;
" nobody has sat there this many a day,
and the room smokes, for the daws have
built in the chimney this spring, and there
were no young men about the Hall to pull
them down."

" Our ain reek's better than other folks'
fire," said Andrew ; " his honour likes the
library. He's nane o' your Papishers, that
delight in blinded ignorance, Mr Syddall."

Very reluctantly, as it appeared to me;
the butler led the way to the library, and,
contrary to what he had given me to expect, the interior of the apartment looked
as if it had been lately arranged, and made
more comfortable than usual. There was
a fire in the grate, which burned clearly,
notwithstanding what Syddall had reported
of the vent. Taking up the tongs, as if to ar-
range the wood, but rather perhaps to con-
ceal his own confusion, the butler observed, " it was burning clear now, but had
smoked woundily in the morning."

Wishing to be alone, till I recovered myself from the first painful sensations which
every thing around me recalled, I desired
old Syddall to call the land-steward, who
lived at about a quarter of a mile from the
Hall. He departed with obvious reluctance. I next ordered Andrew to procure

3

the attendance of a couple of stout fellows upon whom he could rely, the population around being papists, and Sir Rashleigh, who was capable of any desperate enterprize, being in the neighbourhood. Andrew Fairservice undertook this task with great cheerfulness, and promised to bring me up from Trinlay-Knowe, "twa true-blue presbyterians like himsell, that would face and out-face baith the pope, the devil, and the pretender—and blythe will I be o' that company mysell, for the very last night that I was at Osbaldistone-Hall, the blight be on ilka blossom in my bit yard, if I didna see that very picture (pointing to the full-length portrait of Miss Vernon's grandfather) walking by moonlight in the garden! I tauld your honour I was fleyed wi' a bogle that night, but ye wadna listen to me—I aye thought there was witchcraft and devilry amang the papishers, but I ne'er saw't wi' bodily een till that awfu' night."

"Get along, sir," said I, "and bring the fellows you talk of; and see they have

4

more sense than yourself, and are not
frightened at their own shadow."

" I hae been counted as gude a man as
my neighbours ere now," said Andrew, pe-
tulantly ; " but I dinna pretend to deal wi'
evil spirits ;" so made his exit as Wardlaw
the land-steward made his appearance.

He was a man of sense and honesty,
without whose careful management my
uncle would have found it difficult to have
maintained himself a house-keeper so long
as he did. He examined the nature of my
right of possession carefully, and admitted
it candidly. To any one else the succession
would have been a poor one, so much was
the land encumbered with debt and mort-
gage. Most of these, however, were already vested in my father's person, and he
was in a train of acquiring the rest; his
large gains, by the recent rise of the funds,
having made it a matter of ease and convenience for him to pay off the debt which
affected his patrimony.

I transacted much necessary business
with Mr Wardlaw, and detained him to
dine with me. We preferred taking our
repast in the library, although Syddall
strongly recommended our removing to
the Stone-Hall, which he had put in order
for the occasion. Meantime Andrew made
his appearance with his true-blue recruits,
whom he recommended in the highest
terms, as " sober decent men, weel founded in doctrinal points, and, above all, as
bold as lions." I ordered them something
to drink, and they left the room. I observed old Syddall shake his head as they
went out, and insisted upon knowing the
reason.

" I maybe cannot expect," he said, " that
your honour should put confidence in what
I say, but it is Heaven's truth for all that—
Ambrose Wingfield is as honest a man as
lives, but if there is a false knave in the
country, it is his brother Lancie—the whole
country knows him to be a spy for Clerk

Jobson on the poor gentlemen that have
been in trouble—But he's a dissenter, and
I suppose that's enough now-a-days."

Having thus far given vent to his feelings, to which, however, I was little disposed to pay attention, and having placed
the wine on the table, the old butler left
the apartment.

Mr Wardlaw having remained with me
until the evening was somewhat advanced,
at length bundled up his papers, and removed himself to his own habitation, leaving me in that confused state of mind in
which we can hardly say whether we desire
company or solitude. I had not, however,
the choice betwixt them; for I was left
alone in the room, of all others most calculated to inspire me with melancholy reflections.

As twilight was darkening the apartment, Andrew had the sagacity to advance
his head at the door, not to ask if I wished for lights, but to recommend them as a
measure of precaution against the bogles

which still haunted his imagination. I rejected his proffer somewhat peevishly, trimmed the wood fire, and placing myself in one of the large leathern chairs which flanked the old Gothic chimney, I watched unconsciously the bickering of the blaze which I had fostered. " And this," said I alone, " is the progress and the issue of human wishes! nursed by the merest trifles, they are first kindled by fancy, nay, are fed upon the vapour of hope till they consume the substance which they inflame, and man, and his hopes, passions, and desires, sink into a worthless heap of embers and ashes."

There was a deep sigh from the opposite side of the room, which seemed to reply to my reflections. I started up in amazement—Diana Vernon stood before me, resting on the arm of a figure so strongly resembling that of the portrait so often mentioned, that I looked hastily at the frame, expecting to see it empty. My first idea was, either that I had gone suddenly distracted, or that the spirits of the dead had arisen and been placed before me. A second glance convinced me of my being in my senses, and that the forms which stood before me were real and substantial. It was Diana herself, though paler and thinner than her former self; and it was no tenant of the grave who stood beside her, but Vaughan, or rather Sir Frederick Vernon, in a dress made to imitate that of his ancestor, to whose picture his countenance possessed a family resemblance. ⸱ He was the first that spoke, for Diana kept her eyes fast fixed on the ground, and astonishment actually rivetted my tongue to the roof of my mouth.

"We are your suppliants, Mr Osbaldistone," he said, " and we claim the refuge and protection of your roof till we can pursue a journey where dungeons and death gape for me at every step."

" Surely," I articulated with great difficulty—" Miss Vernon cannot suppose—you, sir, cannot believe that I have forgot your interference in my difficulties, or that

I am capable of betraying any one, much less you ?"

" I know it," said Sir Frederick ; " yet it is with the most inexpressible reluctance that I impose on you a confidence, disagreeable perhaps—certainly dangerous—and which I would have specially wished to have conferred on some one else. But my fate, which has chased me through a life of perils and escapes, is now pressing me hard, and I have no alternative,"

At this moment the door opened, and the voice of the officious Andrew was heard. " A'm bringing in the caunles—Ye can light them gin ye like—Can do is easy carried about wi' ane."

I ran to the door, which, as I hoped, I reached in time to prevent his observing who were in the apartment. I turned him out with hasty violence, shut the door after him, and locked it—then instantly remembering his two companions below, knowing his talkative humour, and recollecting Syddall's remark, that one of them was supposed to be a spy, I followed him as fast as I could to the servants' hall, in which they were assembled.   Andrew's tongue was loud as I opened the door, but my unexpected appearance silenced him.

" What is the matter with you, you fool ?" said I ; " you stare and look wild, as if you had seen a ghost."

" N—n—no—nothing," said Andrew ; " but your worship was pleased to be hasty."

" Because you disturbed me out of a sound sleep, you fool.   Syddall tells me he cannot find beds for these good fellows to-night, and Mr Wardlaw thinks there will be no occasion to detain them.   Here is a crown piece for them to drink my health, and thanks for their good will.   You will leave the Hall immediately, my good lads."

The men thanked me for my bounty, took the silver, and withdrew, apparently unsuspicious and contented.   I watched their departure until I was sure they could have no further intercourse that night with honest Andrew. And so instantly had I followed on his heels, that I thought he could not have time to speak two words with them before I interrupted him. But it is wonderful what mischief may be done by only two words. On this occasion they cost two lives.

Having made these arrangements, the best which occurred to me upon the pres-sure of the moment to secure privacy for my guests, I returned to report my pro-ceedings, and added, that I had desired Syddall to answer every summons, conclu-ding that it was by his connivance they had been secreted in the Hall. Diana rai-sed her eyes to thank me for the caution.

" You now understand my mystery," she said ; " you know, doubtless, how near and dear that relative is who has so often found shelter here ; and will be no longer surpri-sed, that Rashleigh, having such a secret at his command, should rule me with a rod of iron."

Her father added, " that it was their intention to trouble me with their presence
as short a time as was possible."

I entreated the fugitives to waive every
consideration but what affected their safety,
and to rely on my utmost exertions to pro-
mote it. This led to an explanation of
the circumstances under which they stood.

" I always suspected Rashleigh Osbaldistone," said Sir Frederick ; " but his conduct towards my unprotected child, which
with difficulty I wrung from her, and his
treachery in your father's affairs, made me
hate and despise him. In our last interview I concealed not my sentiments, as
I should in prudence have attempted ; and
in resentment of the scorn with which I
treated him, he added treachery and apos-
tacy to his catalogue of crimes. I at that
time fondly hoped that his defection would
be of little consequence. The Earl of Marr.
had a gallant army in Scotland, and Lord
Derwentwater, with Forster, Kenmore, Win-
ton, and others, were assembling forces on

the Border. As my connections with these English nobility and gentry were extensive, it was judged proper that I should accompany a detachment of Highlanders, who, under Brigadier MacIntosh of Borlum, crossed the Frith of Forth, traversed the low country of Scotland, and united themselves on the Borders with the English insurgents. My daughter accompanied me through the perils and fatigues of a march so long and difficult."

" And she will never leave her dear father !" exclaimed Miss Vernon, clinging fondly to his arm.

" I had hardly joined our English friends, when I became sensible that our cause was lost. Our numbers diminished instead of increasing, nor were we joined by any except of our own persuasion. The Tories of the High Church remained in general undecided, and at length we were cooped up by a superior force in the little town of Preston. We defended ourselves resolutely one day. On the next, the hearts of our

leaders failed, and they resolved to surrender at discretion. To yield myself up on
such terms, were to have laid my head on
the block. About twenty or thirty gentlemen were of my mind: We mounted our
horses, and placed my daughter, who insisted on sharing my fate, in the centre of
our little party. My companions, struck
with her courage and filial piety, declared
that they would die rather than leave her
behind. We rode in a body down a street
called Fishergate, which leads to a marshy
ground or meadow, extending to the river
Ribble, through which one of our party
promised to show us a good ford. This
marsh had not been strongly invested by
the enemy, so that we had only an affair with
a patrole of Honeywood's dragoons, whom
we dispersed and cut to pieces. We crossed
the river,—gained the high road to Liver-
pool, and then dispersed to seek several
places of concealment and safety. My fortune led me to Wales, where there are many
gentlemen of my religious and political opi-

nions. I could not, however, find a safe opportunity of escaping by sea, and found
myself obliged again to draw towards the
North. A well-tried friend has appointed
to meet me in this neighbourhood, and
guide me to a sea-port on the Solway, where
a sloop is prepared to carry me from my
native country for ever. As Osbaldistone-
Hall was for the present uninhabited, and
under the charge of old Syddall, who had
been our confidant on former occasions, we
drew to it as to a place of known and secure refuge. I resumed a dress which had
been used with good effect to scare the superstitious rustics, or domestics, who chanced at any time to see me; and we expected from time to time to hear by Syddall of
the arrival of our friendly guide, when your
sudden coming hither, and occupying this
apartment, laid us under the necessity of
submitting to your mercy."

Thus ended Sir Frederick's story, whose
tale sounded to me like one told in a vi-
sion; and I could hardly bring myself to

believe, that I saw his daughter's form once more before me in flesh and blood, though with diminished beauty and sunk spirits. The buoyant vivacity with which she had resisted every touch of adversity, had now assumed the air of composed and submissive, but dauntless resolution and constancy. Her father, though aware and jealous of the effect of her praises on my mind, could not forbear expatiating upon them.

" She has endured trials," he said, " which might have dignified the history of a martyr ;—she has faced danger and death in various shapes ;—she has undergone toil and privation, from which men of the strongest frame would have shrunk ;—she has spent the day in darkness, and the night in vigil, and has never breathed a murmur of weakness or complaint. In a word, Mr Osbaldistone," he concluded, "she is a worthy offering to that God to whom," crossing himself, " I shall dedicate her, as all that is left dear or precious to Frederick Vernon."

There was a silence after these words, of

which I well understood the mournful import. The father of Diana was still as anxious to destroy my hopes of being united to
her now, as he had shown himself during
our brief meeting in Scotland.

" We will now," said he to his daughter,
" intrude no farther on Mr Osbaldistone's
time, since we have acquainted him with
the circumstances of the miserable guests
who claim his protection."

I requested them to stay, and offered
myself to leave the apartment. Sir Frederick observed, that my doing so could not
but excite my attendant's suspicion ; and
that the place of their retreat was in every
respect commodious, and furnished by Syddall with all they could possibly want.
" We might possibly have even contrived
to remain there from your observation ;
but it would have been unjust to decline
the most absolute reliance on your honour."

" You have done me but justice," I re-
replied. " To you, Sir Frederick, I am

but little known; but Miss Vernon, I am sure, will bear me witness that"——

" I do not want my daughter's evidence," he said politely, but yet with an air calcu- lated to prevent my addressing myself to Diana, " since I am prepared to believe all that is worthy of Mr Francis Osbaldistone. Permit us now to retire; we must take re- pose when we can, since we are absolutely uncertain when we may be called upon to renew our perilous journey."

He drew his daughter's arm within his, and, with a profound reverence, disappear- ed with her behind the tapestry.

CHAPTER XII.

But now the hand of fate is on the curtain,
And gives the scene to light.

                              DON SEBASTIAN.

I FELT stunned and chilled as they retired. Imagination, dwelling on an absent
object of affection, paints her not only in the
fairest light, but in that in which we most
desire to behold her. I had thought of
Diana as she was, when her parting tear
dropped on my cheek; when her parting token, received from the wife of Mac-
Gregor, augured her wish to convey into
exile and conventical seclusion the remembrance of my affection. I saw her; and
her cold passive manner, expressive of little, except composed melancholy, disap-

pointed, and, in some degree, almost offended me. In the egotism of my feelings, I accused her of indifference—of insensibility. I upbraided her father with pride, with cruelty, with fanaticism ; forgetting that both were sacrificing their interest, and Diana her inclination, to the discharge of what they regarded as their duty.

Sir Frederick Vernon was a rigid Catholic, who thought the path of salvation too narrow to be trodden by an heretic ; and Diana, to whom her father's safety had been for many years the principal and moving spring of thoughts, hopes, and actions, felt that she had discharged her duty in resigning to his will, not alone her property in the world, but the dearest affections of her heart. But it was not surprising that I could not, at such a moment, fully appreciate these honourable motives ; yet my spleen sought no ignoble means of discharging itself.

"I am contemned, then," said I, when

left to run over the tenor of Sir Frederick's communications, " I am contemned, and thought unworthy even to exchange words with her. Be it so ; they shall not at least prevent me from watching over her safety. Here will I remain as an out-post, and, while under my roof at least, no danger shall threaten her, if it be such as the arm of one determined man can avert."

- I summoned Syddall to the library. He came, but came attended by the eternal Andrew, who, dreaming of great things in consequence of my taking possession of the Hall and the annexed estates, was re-solved to lose nothing for want of keeping himself in view ; and, as often happens to men who entertain selfish objects, overshot his mark, and rendered his attentions te-dious and inconvenient.

His unrequired presence prevented me from speaking freely to Syddall, and I dared not send him away for fear of increasing such suspicions as he might entertain from his former abrupt dismissal from the library.

" I shall sleep here, sir," I said, giving
them directions to wheel nearer to the fire
an old-fashioned day-bed, or settee. " I
have much to do, and shall go late to bed."

Syddall, who seemed to understand my
look, offered to procure me the accommodation of a mattress and some bedding. I
accepted his offer, dismissed my attendant,
lighted a pair of candles, and desired that
I might not be disturbed till seven in the
ensuing morning.

The domestics retired, leaving me to my
painful and ill-arranged reflections, until
nature, worn out, should require some repose.

I endeavoured forcibly to abstract my
mind from the singular circumstances in
which I found myself placed. Feelings
which I had gallantly combatted while the
exciting object was remote, were now exas-
perated by my immediate neighbourhood
to her whom I was so soon to part with for
ever. Her name was written in every book
which I attempted to peruse ; and her image

forced itself on me in whatever train of thought I strove to engage myself. It was like the officious slave of Prior's Solomon,—

> Abra was ready ere I named her name,
> And when I called another, Abra came.

I alternately gave way to these thoughts, and struggled against them, sometimes yielding to a mood of melting tenderness of sorrow which was scarce natural to me, sometimes arming myself with the hurt pride of one who had experienced what he esteemed unmerited rejection. I paced the library until I had chafed myself into a temporary fever. I then threw myself on the couch, and endeavoured to compose myself to sleep; but it was in vain that I used every effort to compose myself—that I lay without movement of finger or of muscle, as still as if I had been already a corpse—that I endeavoured to divert or banish disquieting thoughts, by fixing my mind on some act of repetition or arithmetical process. My blood throbbed to my feverish apprehension in pulsations which resembled the deep and regular stroke of a distant fulling-mill, and tingled in my veins like streams of liquid fire.

At length I arose, opened the window, and stood by it for some time in the clear moonlight, receiving, in part at least, that refreshment and dissipation of ideas from the clear and calm scene, without which they had become beyond the command of my own volition. I resumed my place on the couch with a heart, heaven knows, not lighter, but firmer, and more resolved for endurance. In a short time a slumber crept over my senses ; still, however, though my senses slumbered, my soul was awake to the painful feelings of my situation, and my dreams were of mental anguish and ex- ternal objects of terror.

I remember a strange agony, under which I conceived myself and Diana in the power of MacGregor's wife, and about to be precipitated from a rock into the lake ; the signal was to be the discharge of a cannon, fired by Sir Frederick Vernon, who, in the dress of a cardinal, officiated at the ceremony. Nothing could be more lively than the impression which I received of this imaginary scene. I could paint, even at this moment, the mute and courageous submission expressed in Diana's features— the wild and distorted faces of the executioners, who crowded around us with " mopping and mowing ;" grimaces ever changing, and each more hideous than that which preceded. I saw the rigid and inflexible fanaticism painted in the face of the father—I saw him lift the fatal match —the deadly signal exploded—It was repeated again and again and again, in rival thunders, by the echoes of the surrounding cliffs, and I awoke from fancied horror to real apprehension.

The sounds in my dream were not ideal. They reverberated on my waking ears, but it was two or three minutes ere I could collect myself so as distinctly to understand that they proceeded from a violent knocking at the gate. I leaped from my couch in great apprehension, took my sword under my arm, and hastened to forbid the admission of any one. But my route was necessarily circuitous, because the library looked not upon the quadrangle, but into the gardens. When I had reached a staircase, the windows of which looked into the entrance court, I heard the feeble and intimidated tones of Syddall expostulating with rough voices, which demanded admittance, by the warrant of Justice Standish, and in the King's name, and threatened the old domestic with the heaviest penal consequences, if he refused instant obedience. Ere they had ceased, I heard, to my unspeakable provocation, the voice of Andrew bidding Syddall stand aside, and let him open the door.

"If they come in King George's name we have naething to fear—we hae spent baith bluid and gowd for him—We dinna need to darn ourselves like some folks, Mr

Syddall—We are neither Papists nor Jacobites, I trow."

It was in vain I accelerated my pace down
stairs ; I heard bolt after bolt withdrawn by
the officious scoundrel, while all the time
he was boasting his own and his master's
loyalty to King George ; and I could easily calculate that the party must enter
before I could arrive at the door to re-
place the bars. Devoting the back of Andrew Fairservice to the cudgel so soon as
I should have time to pay him his deserts,
I ran back to the library, barricaded the
door as I best could, and hastened to
that by which Diana and her father entered, and begged for instant admittance.
Diana herself undid the door. She was
ready dressed, and betrayed neither perturbation nor fear.

" Danger is so familiar to us," she said,
" that we are always prepared to meet it—
My father is already up—he is in Rashleigh's apartment—We will escape into the

garden, and thence by the postern-gate (I have the key from Syddall in case of need) into the wood—I know its dingles better than any one now alive—Keep them a few minutes in play.—And, dear, dear Frank, once more, fare you well!"

She vanished like a meteor to join her father, and the intruders were rapping violently, and attempting to force the library door by the time I had returned into it.

"You robber dogs!" I exclaimed, wilfully mistaking the purpose of their disturbance, "if you do not instantly quit the house I will fire my blunderbuss through the door."

"Fire a fool's bauble!" said Andrew Fairservice; "it's Mr Clerk Jobson, with a legal warrant"——

"To search for, take, and apprehend," said the voice of that execrable pettifogger, "the bodies of certain persons in my warrant named, charged of high treason under the 13th of King William, chapter third."

And the violence on the door was re-
newed. " I am rising, gentlemen," said I,
desirous to gain as much time as possible
—" commit no violence—give me leave to
look at your warrant; and, if it is formal
and legal, I shall not oppose it."

" God save great George our King!"
ejaculated Andrew. " I tauld ye you
would find no Jacobites here."

Spinning out the time as much as possible, I was at length compelled to open
the door, which they would otherwise have
forced.

Mr Jobson entered, with several assistants, among whom I discovered the younger Wingfield, to whom, doubtless, he was
obliged for his information, and exhibited
his warrant, directed not only against Frederick Vernon, an attainted traitor, but
also against Diana Vernon, spinster, and
Francis Osbaldistone, gentleman, accused
of misprision of treason. It was a case in
which resistance would have been madness ; I therefore, after capitulating for a

few minutes delay, surrendered myself a prisoner.

I had next the mortification to see Jobson go straight to the chamber of Miss Vernon, and I learned that from thence, without hesitation or difficulty, he went to the room where Sir Frederick had slept. " The hare has stolen away," said the brute, " but her form is warm—the greyhounds will have her by the haunches yet."

A scream from the garden announced that he prophesied too truly. In the course of five minutes, Rashleigh entered the library with Sir Frederick Vernon and his daughter as prisoners. " The fox," he said, " knew his old earth, but he forgot it could be stopped by a careful huntsman—I had not forgot the garden gate, Sir Frederick —or, if that title suits you better, Most Noble Lord Beauchamp."

" Rashleigh," said Sir Frederick, " thou art a detestable villain !"

" I better deserved the name, Sir Knight,

or my Lord, when, under the direction of an able tutor, I sought to introduce civil war into the bosom of a peaceful country. But I have done my best," said he, looking upwards, " to atone for my errors."

. I could hold no longer. I had designed to watch their proceedings in silence, but I felt that I must speak or die. " If hell," I said, " has one complexion more hideous than another, it is where villainy is masked by hypocrisy."

" Ha ! my gentle cousin," said Rashleigh, holding a candle towards me, and surveying me from head to foot ; " right welcome to Osbaldistone-Hall—I can forgive your spleen—It is hard to lose an estate and a mistress in one night ; for we shall take possession of this poor manorhouse in the name of the lawful heir, Sir Rashleigh Osbaldistone."

While Rashleigh braved it out in this manner, I could see that he put a strong force upon his feelings, both of anger and shame. But his state of mind was more obvious when Diana Vernon addressed him. " Rashleigh," she said, " I pity you —for, deep as the evil is you have labour-ed to do me, and the evil you have actual-ly done, I cannot hate you so much as I scorn and pity you. What you have now done may be the work of an hour, but will furnish you with reflection for your life— of what nature I leave to your own con-science, which will not slumber for ever."

Rashleigh strode once or twice through the room, came up to the side-table, on which wine was still standing, and poured out a large glass with a trembling hand; but when he saw that we observed his tre-mor, he suppressed it by a strong effort, and, looking at us with fixed and daring composure, carried the bumper to his head without spilling a drop.

" It is my father's old burgundy," he said, looking to Jobson; " I am glad there is some of it left—You will get proper persons to take care of the house and

8

property in my name, and turn out the do-
ting old butler, and that foolish Scotch
rascal. Meanwhile, we will convey these
persons to a more proper place of custody.—I have provided the old family-coach
for your convenience," he said, " though
I am not ignorant that even the lady could
brave the night-air on foot or on horseback, were the errand more to her mind."

Andrew wrung his hands.—" I only said
that my master was surely speaking to a
ghaist in the library—and the villain Lancie to betray an auld friend that sang aff
the same Psalm-book wi' him every Sunday
for twenty years."

He was turned out of the house, together with Syddall, without allowing him to
conclude his lamentation. His expulsion,
however, led to some singular consequences. Resolving, according to his own story, to go down for the night where mother Simpson would give him a lodging
for old acquaintance sake, he had just got

clear of the avenue, and into the old wood
as it was called, though it was now used
as pasture-ground rather than woodland,
when he suddenly lighted on a drove of
Scotch cattle, which were lying there to
repose themselves after the day's journey.
At this, Andrew was in no way surprised,
it being the well-known custom of his countrymen, who take care of those droves, to
quarter themselves after night upon the
best uninclosed grass-ground they can
find, and depart before day-break to escape
paying for their night's lodgings. But he
was both surprised and startled, when a
Highlander starting up, accused him of
disturbing the cattle, and refused him to
pass forward till he had spoken to his master. The mountaineer conducted Andrew
into a thicket, where he found three or
four more of his countrymen. " And,"
said Andrew, " I saw sune they were ower
mony men for the drove; and from the
questions they put to me, I judged they
had other tow on their rock."

5

They questioned him closely about all
that had passed at Osbaldistone-Hall, and
seemed surprised and concerned at the report he made to them.

" And troth," said Andrew, " I tauld
them a' I kenn'd ; for dirks and pistols
were what I could never refuse information
to in all my life."

They talked in whispers among themselves, and at length collected their cattle
together, and drove them close up to the
entrance of the avenue, which might be
half a mile distant from the house. They
proceeded to drag together some felled
trees, which lay in the vicinity, so as to
make a temporary barricade across the road,
about fifteen yards beyond the avenue. It
was now near day-break, and there was a
pale eastern gleam mingled with the fading
moonlight, so that objects could be discovered with some distinctness. The lum-
bering sound of a coach, drawn by four
horses, and escorted by six men on horseback, was heard coming up the avenue.

The Highlanders listened attentively. The carriage contained Mr Jobson and his unfortunate prisoners. The escort consisted of Rashleigh, and several horsemen, peace-officers and their assistants. So soon as we had passed the gate at the head of the avenue, it was shut behind the cavalcade by a Highlandman, stationed there for that purpose. At the same time, the carriage was impeded in its farther progress by the cattle, amongst whom we were involved, and by the barricade in front. Two of the escort dismounted to remove the felled trees, which they might think were left there by accident or carelessness. The others began with their whips to drive the cattle from the road.

"Who dare abuse our cattle?" said a rough voice.—"Shoot him, Angus."

Rashleigh instantly called out, "A rescue—a rescue!" and firing a pistol, wounded the man who spoke.

"*Claymore!*" cried the leader of the Highlanders, and a scuffle instantly commenced.

The officers of the law, surprised at so sudden an attack, and not usually possessing the most desperate bravery, made but an imperfect defence, considering the superiority of their numbers. Some attempted to ride back to the Hall, but on a pistol being fired from behind the gate, they conceived themselves surrounded, and at length gallopped off in different directions. Rashleigh, meanwhile, had dismounted, and on foot had maintained a desperate and single-handed conflict with the leader of the band. The window of the carriage, on my side, permitted me to witness it. At length Rashleigh dropped.

" Will you ask forgiveness for the sake of God, King James, and auld friendship ?" said a voice which I knew right well.

" No, never," said Rashleigh, firmly.

" Then, traitor, die in your treason !" retorted MacGregor, and plunged his sword in his prostrate antagonist.

In the next moment he was at the carriage door—handed out Miss Vernon, assisted her father and me to alight, and dragging out the attorney, head foremost, threw him under the wheel.

" Mr Osbaldistone," he said, in a whisper, " you have nothing to fear—I must look after those who have—Your friends will soon be in safety—Farewell, and forget not the MacGregor."

He whistled—his band gathered round him, and, hurrying Diana and her father along with him, they were almost instantly lost in the glades of the forest. The coachman and postillion had abandoned their horses, and fled at the first discharge of fire-arms; but the animals, stopped by the barricade, remained perfectly still; and well for Jobson that they did so, for the slightest motion would have dragged the wheel over his body. My first object was to relieve him, for such was the rascal's terror that he never could have risen by his own exertions. I next commanded him to observe, that I had neither taken part in the rescue, nor availed myself

of it to make my escape, and enjoined him
to go down to the Hall, and call some of
his party, who had been left there, to assist the wounded. But Jobson's fears had
so mastered and controuled every faculty
of his mind, that he was totally incapable
of moving. I now resolved to go myself,
but in my way stumbled over the body of
a man, as I thought dead or dying. It
was, however, Andrew Fairservice, as well
and whole as ever he was in his life, who
had only taken this recumbent posture to
avoid the slashes, stabs, and pistol-balls,
which, for a moment or two, were flying in
various directions. I was so glad to find
him that I did not enquire how he came
thither, but instantly commanded his assistance.

Rashleigh was our first object—He groaned when I approached him, as much through
spite as through pain, and shut his eyes, as
if determined, like Iago, to speak no word
more. We lifted him into the carriage, and
performed the same good office to another

wounded man, who had been left on the field. I then with difficulty made Jobson understand that he must enter the coach also, and support Sir Rashleigh upon the seat. He obeyed, but with an air as if he but half comprehended my meaning. Andrew and I turned the horses' heads round, and opening the gate of the avenue, led them slowly back to Osbaldistone-Hall.

Some fugitives had already reached the Hall by circuitous routes, and alarmed its garrison by the news that Sir Rashleigh, Clerk Jobson, and all their escort, save they who escaped to tell the tale, had been cut to pieces, at the head of the avenue, by a whole regiment of wild Highlanders. When we reached the mansion, therefore, we heard such a buzz as arises when bees are alarmed, and mustering in their hives. Mr Jobson, however, who had now in some measure come to his senses, found voice enough to make himself known. He was the more anxious to be released from the carriage, as one of his companions (the peace-officer,)

had, to his inexpressible terror, expired by
his side with a hideous groan.

Sir Rashleigh Osbaldistone was still alive, ·
but so dreadfully wounded that the bottom
of the coach was filled with his blood, and
long traces of it left from the entrance-door
into the Stone-Hall, where he was placed in
a chair, some attempting to stop the bleeding with cloths, while others called for a
surgeon, and no one seemed willing to go
to fetch one.

"Torment me not," said the wounded
man. "I know no assistance can avail
me. I am a dying man." He raised himself in his chair, though the damps and fer-
vour of death were already on his brow,
and spoke with a firmness which seemed
beyond his strength. "Cousin Francis,"
he said, "draw near to me." I approached him as he requested.—"I wish you only
to know that the pangs of death do not al-
ter one iota of my feeling towards you. I
hate you!" he said, the expression of rage
throwing a hideous glare into the eyes
which were soon to be closed for ever—"I

hate you with a hatred as intense, now while I lie bleeding before you, as if my foot trode on your neck."

"I have given you no cause, sir; and for your own sake I could wish your mind in a better temper."

"You *have* given me cause," he rejoined—"in love, in ambition, in the paths of interest, you have crossed and blighted me at every turn. I was born to be the honour of my father's house—I have been its disgrace—and all owing to you.—My very patrimony has become your's—Take it," he said, "and may the curse of a dying man cleave to it!"

In a moment after he had uttered this frightful wish, he fell back in the chair; his eyes became glazed, his limbs stiffened, but the grin and glare of mortal hatred survived even the last gasp of life. I will dwell no longer on so hideous a picture, nor say any more of the death of Rashleigh, than that it gave me access to my rights of inheritance without farther challenge, and that Jobson found himself compelled to allow, that the ridiculous charge of misprision of high-treason was only made to favour Rashleigh's views, and remove me from Osbaldistone-Hall. The rascal's name was struck off the list of attornies, and he was reduced to poverty and contempt.

I returned to London when I had put my affairs in order at Osbaldistone-Hall, and felt happy to escape from a place which suggested so many painful recollections. My anxiety was now acute to learn the fate of Diana and her father. A French gentleman, who came to London on commercial business, was entrusted with a letter to me from Miss Vernon, which put my mind at rest respecting their safety.

It gave me to understand, that the opportune appearance of MacGregor and his party was not fortuitous. The Scottish nobles and gentry, engaged in the insurrection, as well as those of England, were particularly anxious to further the escape of Sir Frederick Vernon, who, as an old and trusted agent of the house of Stuart, was possessed of matter enough to have ruined

half Scotland. Rob Roy, of whose sagacity and courage they had known so many
proofs, was the person whom they pitched
upon to assist his escape, and the place of
meeting was fixed at Osbaldistone-Hall.
You have already heard how nearly the
plan had been disconcerted by the activity
of the unhappy Rashleigh. It succeeded,
however, perfectly ; for when once Sir Frederick and his daughter were again at large,
·they found horses prepared for them, and
by MacGregor's knowledge of the country,
for every part of Scotland, and of the north
of England, was familiar to him, were conducted to the western sea-coast, and safely
embarked for France. The same gentleman told me, that Sir Frederick was not
expected to survive for many months a
lingering disease, the consequence of late
hardships and privations. His daughter
was placed in a convent, and it was her father's wish she should take the veil, although
he recommended the cloister.

When these news reached me, I frankly

told the state of my affections to my father, who was not a little startled at the idea of my marrying a Roman Catholic. But he was very desirous to see me " settled in life," as he called it ; and he was sensible that, in joining him with heart and hand in his commercial labours, I had sacrificed my own inclinations. After a brief hesitation, and several questions asked and answered to his satisfaction, he broke out with—" I little thought a son of mine should have been Lord of Osbaldistone Manor, and far less that he should go to a French convent for a spouse. But so dutiful a daughter cannot but prove a good wife. You have worked at the desk to please me, Frank ; it is but fair you should wive to please yourself."

How I sped in my wooing, Will Tresham, I need not tell you. You know, too, how long and happily I lived with Diana. You know how I lamented her. But you do not—cannot know how much she deserved her husband's sorrow.

I have no more of romantic adventure to tell, nor indeed any thing to communicate farther, since the latter incidents of my life are so well known to one who has shared, with the most friendly sympathy, the joys, as well as the sorrows, by which its scenes have been chequered. I often visited Scotland, but never again saw the bold Highlander who had such an influence on the early events of my life. I learned, however, from time to time, that he continued to maintain his ground among the mountains of Loch Lomond, in despite of his powerful enemies, and that he even obtained, to a certain degree, the connivance of government to his self-elected office of Protector of the Lennox, in virtue of which he levied black-mail with as much regularity as the proprietors did their ordinary rents. It seemed impossible that his life should have concluded without a violent end. Nevertheless, he died in old age, and by a peaceful death, sometime about the year 1736, and is still remembered in his country as the Robin Hood of Scotland, the dread of the wealthy, but the friend of the poor, and possessed of many qualities, both of head and heart, which would have graced a less equivocal profession than that to which his fate condemned him.

Old Andrew Fairservice, whom you may recollect as gardener at Osbaldistone-Hall, used to say, that " There were many things ower bad for blessing, and ower gude for banning, like Rob Roy."

[Here the original manuscript ends somewhat abruptly. I have reason to think that what followed related to private affairs.]

END OF VOLUME THIRD.

EDINBURGH:
Printed by James Ballantyne & Co.

CPSIA information can be obtained
at www.ICGtesting.com
Printed in the USA
LVHW081031270422
716604LV00100B/207